ADDITIONAL BOOKS
AND
CHRISTIAN CLASSICS

WRITTEN OR EDITED FOR MODERN RELEASE BY

BYRON PERRRINE

Christianity:
What It is and What It Means

Cristianismo:
¿Qué es y qué significa?

Emerson's Evangelical Primer

Christian Unity 101

Extracts from the Religious Works of La Mothe Fenelon

The Religion that Shaped America

Memoir of Catharine Brown

How Can the Sinner Love God's Law?
Universal Atonement, Sin and the Natural Law Explained

A CHRISTIAN CLASSICAL READER FOR THE USE OF CHILDREN AT HOME AND SCHOOL

*Compiled and Edited
with Explanatory Notes*

BY

BYRON PERRRINE

"Every hour in the society of a parent (or teacher) who understands education, and pays proper attention to it, is an hour gained to moral improvement.... In whatever way the child is employed, whether in talking or playing, a moral lesson may be instilled, moral habits may be encouraged, and bad ones repressed.... Thus good will be doing, and a foundation laying for still greater good."

—Thomas Babington

TABLE OF CONTENTS

EDITOR'S NOTE TO PARENTS AND EDUCATORS

T his anthology contains readings representative of the Christian classical curriculum trusted and prized by previous generations of Americans. It is provided as an exemplar for the teaching of reading, faith, and morals, to children and adolescents at home and in the school. In addition to utilizing these materials, it is hoped that you, the reader, will be inspired to embark upon your own journey of exploration and discovery. There are many forgotten curriculum treasures yet to be discovered and reintroduced into modern instruction, too many for all of them to be included in this volume. With but a bit of research on your part, you will find all that is needed to provide the same solid training that was received by the founders of the American republic, and is now waiting to be reintroduced and passed on to future generations of Americans.

In recent decades, there has been a wave of unproductive cultural experimentation resulting in the introduction of secularism in our public schools. Secularism does not mean neutrality toward Christianity. Secularism is hostile toward Christianity. Teaching methods, which aim to cultivate the development of "critical thinking" skills might well be very helpful in our schools, excepting that a bias against Christian epistemology has been grafted onto them. Not only is exposure to Christian and classical values neglected in public schools today, values which for centuries have been the foundation of Western civilization, there is open hostility to Christian and classical values. Can children and adolescents be expected to develop their own healthy moral and ethical society when "critical thinking" which excludes consideration of Christian epistemology and classical virtues is being taught? Are children and adolescents expected to "re-invent the wheel" in a vacuum? Of course not! The result of such folly is seen in the rise of an increasingly uncivil and dysfunctional "me-first", "values-neutral" society, and, in the politics of resentment. Depriving children and adolescents of exposure to the rich moral and ethical traditions of Western Civilization is leading to tragic and unfortunate results for young adults personally, and for American society as a whole. It is time for change.

Those advocating a "values neutral" educational system which excludes the Christian classical perspective have, in effect, put blinders on our children, depriving them of a curriculum that has been tried and held to be true for centuries, the very curriculum upon which America was built. In support of the concept that children and adolescents be encouraged to ask "fresh and original questions about life and its meaning", a concept ostensibly prized by secular educators, let us insist that children's "fresh and original questions" include the option of exploring the timeless questions and answers offered by Christian and classical philosophy! Let the children be set free through exposure to the truth! Let them develop good and responsible study habits which facilitate the joy of academic exploration! Give them the tools and habits necessary for success. Teach them respect for themselves and each other! Let us provide an educational platform for self-determined learning which actually works, a platform for learning that has been proven by centuries of successful trial, and which in every respect is far more legitimate than a so-called "values neutral" curriculum which in fact is not values neutral at all, but is hostile to Christian and classical values.

Please consider the following points made by Joseph Story in his essay titled "Classical Learning", extracted from The American Common-School Reader and Speaker (Boston: Tappan, Whittemore and Mason, 1844). Joseph Story served on the Supreme Court of the United States from 1812 to 1845.

> *The importance of classical learning to professional education, is so obvious, that the surprise is, that it could ever have become matter of disputation. I speak not of its power in refining the taste, in disciplining the judgment, in invigorating the understanding, or in warming the heart with elevated sentiments; but of its power of direct, positive, necessary instruction. Until the eighteenth century, the mass of science, in its principal branches, was deposited in the dead languages, and much of it still reposes there. To be ignorant of these languages, is to shut out the lights of former times, or to examine them only through the glimmerings of inadequate translations.*
>
> *It is often said, that there have been eminent men and eminent writers, to whom the ancient languages were unknown,—men who have risen by the force of their talents, and writers who have written with a purity and ease which*

hold them up, as models for imitation. On the other hand, it is as often said, that scholars do not always compose either with elegance or chasteness; that their diction is sometimes loose and harsh, and sometimes ponderous and affected.

Be it so. I am not disposed to call in question the accuracy of either statement. But I would, nevertheless, say that the presence of classical learning was not the cause of the faults of the one class, nor the absence of it, the cause of the excellence of the other. And I would put this fact, as an answer to all such reasoning, that there is not a single language of modern Europe, in which literature has made any considerable advances, which is not directly of Roman origin, or has not incorporated into its very structure many, very many, of the idioms and peculiarities of the ancient tongues. The English language affords a strong illustration of the truth of this remark. It abounds with words and meanings drawn from classical sources. Innumerable phrases retain the symmetry of their ancient dress. Innumerable expressions have received their vivid tints from the beautiful dyes of Roman and Grecian roots. If scholars, therefore, do not write our language with ease, or purity, or elegance, the cause must lie somewhat deeper than a conjectural ignorance of its true diction.

I repeat, there is not a single nation from the north to the south of Europe, from the bleak shores of the Baltic to the bright plains of immortal Italy, whose literature is not imbedded in the very elements of classical learning. The literature of England is, in an emphatic sense, the production of her scholars, of men who have cultivated letters in her universities, and colleges, and grammar schools, of men who thought any life too short, chiefly because it left some relic of antiquity un-mastered, and any other fame humble, because it faded in the presence of Roman and Grecian genius.

He who studies English literature without the lights of classical learning, loses half the charms of its sentiments and style, of its force and feelings, of its delicate touches, of its delightful allusions, of its illustrative associations. Who that reads the poetry of Gray, does not feel that it is the refinement of classical taste, which gives such inexpressible vividness and transparency to his diction? Who that reads the concentrated sense and melodious versification of Dryden and Pope, does not perceive in them the disciples of the old school, whose genius was inflamed by the heroic verse, the terse satire, and the playful wit of antiquity? Who that meditates over the strains of Milton does not feel that he drank deep at "Siloa's brook, that flowed fast by the oracle of God;" that the fires of his magnificent mind were lighted by coals from ancient altars?

It is no exaggeration to declare, that he who proposes to abolish classical studies, proposes to render, in a great measure, inert and unedifying the mass of English literature for three centuries; to rob us of much of the glory of the past, and much of the instruction of future ages; to blind us to excellences which few may hope to equal, and none to surpass; to annihilate associations which are interwoven with our best sentiments, and give to distant times and countries a presence and reality, as if they were, in fact, our own.

I would also commend to your attention, "The Bible the Best Classic", by Thomas S. Grimke, American attorney, author, orator, and social activist (1786-1834). This article appeared in <u>McGuffy's Fifth Eclectic Reader</u> of 1879, and, in Ebenezer Porter's <u>The Rhetorical Reader</u> of 1835, from which the following is drawn:

To the Parent, I would say, your offspring are the children of God. On you they depend for education. God has commanded you to train them betimes, to know and to serve, to love and to enjoy him. The paths of business are equally the paths of temptation and duty. Religion belongs to every thought, and word, and deed. As then the Bible is the only standard of duty, why do you not interweave it with the whole scheme of secular education? To the Instructor, I would say, you stand in the place of Parent and Guardian. Their duties are unquestionably yours. To you is transferred, not only the obligation to teach, but more especially the selection of appropriate books, and the regulation of the order and proportion of studies. What Parent or Guardian has over interfered with your plans? How entirely, and with what a cordial confidence, have they appointed you to think, to consult, to decide, to act for them? Why then have you excluded the Bible of those very Parents and Guardians, from the whole scheme for the education of their children and wards? To the Patriot, I would say, can you doubt, that to the Bible, your country owes not only her religious liberty, and her entire moral condition, but to a great extent, her civil and political rights, her science, literature and arts? The Bible is emphatically the book of truth and knowledge, of freedom and happiness to your country. Children you regard as public property; and you know, that they will honor and serve their country best, the more they are instructed in the Scriptures, and imbued with their spirit. Why then, do you withhold the full benefit of those sacred oracles, by thus proscribing them, in every scheme of education? To the Christian, I would say, you admit the divinity of the Scriptures, their absolute authority and inestimable worth. You concede, that they are the common property of all; that even children may profit by them, since they are so simple and plain, that the wayfaring man, though a fool, shall not err therein. Why then do you not give them this lamp of life, as well as the lamp of knowledge to guide them daily, with harmonious beams, in their preparation for the inseparable duties and business of life. To the Scholar, I would say, we offer you a more ancient, venerable, noble classic, than is to be found in the whole compass, of Grecian and Roman Literature.

Regarding suitable instructional methodology, there is no need to labor over the seemingly endless new instructional theories which vie for your attention today, most of which deprive the student of a rich and solidly grounded moral education. Do you wish to be a successful Christian parent or teacher? Read *A Practical View of Christian Education in its Earliest Stages* by Thomas Babington. Obtain this book, read it, and internalize its principles. Afterwards, if you have time, you may wish to consider additional instructional theories and practices, but I think this one book provides a sufficient foundation for success.

Not that all educational innovation is harmful. Gleaning additional ideas from, for example, Matthew Lipman and his so-called *Philosophy for Children Movement*, may prove to be enriching, and possibly helpful.

Lipman's hope was that philosophy would acquire a central place in the K-12 curriculum, thus enabling students to develop their reasoning and argumentative skills. First and foremost, however, my dear reader, obtain a copy of Babington's classic. In that rather slim old volume, you will find guidance sufficient for you as parents and educators to become effective in your efforts to encourage the moral and intellectual development of your children and/or students.

—B. Perrine

February 20, 2020

PART I:
SELECTED LESSONS FROM

The American Common-School
Reader and Speaker

Compiled by
John Goldsbury, A. M. and William Russell

Boston:
Tappan, Whittemore and Mason, 1844

LESSON 1:
LOSS OF NATIONAL CHARACTER—MAXCY

The loss of a firm national character, or the degradation of a nation's honor, is the inevitable prelude to her destruction. Behold the once proud fabric of a Roman empire,—an empire carrying its arts and arms, into every part of the eastern continent; the monarchs of mighty kingdoms, dragged at the wheels of her triumphal chariots; her eagle waving over the ruins of desolated countries. Where is her splendor, her wealth, her power, her glory? Extinguished forever. Her moldering temples, the mournful vestiges of her former grandeur, afford a shelter to her muttering monks. Where are her statesmen, her sages, her philosophers, her orators, her generals? Go to their solitary tombs, and inquire. She lost her national character, and her destruction followed. The ramparts of her national pride were broken down, and Vandalism desolated her classic fields.

Citizens will lose their respect and confidence in our government, if it does not extend over them the shield of an honorable national character. Corruption will creep in, and sharpen party animosity. Ambitious leaders will seize upon the favorable moment. The mad enthusiasm for revolution, will call into action the irritate spirit of our nation, and civil war must follow. The swords of our countrymen may yet glitter on our mountains; their blood may yet crimson our plains.

Such,--the warning voice of all antiquity, the example of all republics proclaim,--may be our fate. But let us no longer indulge these gloomy anticipations. The commencement of our liberty, presages the dawn of a brighter period, to the world. That bold, enterprising spirit which conducted our heroes to peace and safety, and gave us a lofty rank amid the empires of the world, still animates the bosoms of their descendants. Look back to that moment, when they unbarred the dungeons of the slave, and dashed his fetters to the earth; when the sword of a Washington leaped from its scabbard, to revenge the slaughter of our countrymen. Place their example before you. Let the sparks of their veteran wisdom flash across your minds, and the sacred altars of your liberty, crowned with immortal honors, rise before you. Relying on the virtue, the courage, the patriotism, and the strength of our country, we may expect our national character will become more energetic, our citizens more enlightened, and may hail the age, as not far distant, when will be heard, as the proudest exclamation of men: "I am an American."

LESSON 2:
RESISTANCE TO OPPRESSION
—PATRICK HENRY

Mr. President,—It is natural for man to indulge in the illusions of hope. We are apt to shut our eyes against a painful truth, and listen to the song of the siren, till she transforms us into beasts. Is this the part of wise men engaged in a great and arduous struggle for liberty? Are we disposed to be of the number of those, who, having eyes, see not, and having ears, hear not, the things which so nearly concern their temporal salvation? For my part, whatever anguish of spirit it may cost, I am willing to know the whole truth; to know the worst, and to provide for it.

I have but one lamp, by which my feet are guided; and that is the lamp of experience. I know of no way of judging of the future by the past. And judging by the past, I wish to know what there is in the conduct of the British ministry, or the last ten years, to justify those hopes with which gentlemen have been pleased to solace themselves and the House? Is it that insidious smile, with which our petition has been lately received? Trust it no, sir; it will prove a snare to your feet. Suffer not yourselves to be betrayed with a kiss.

Ask yourselves how this gracious reception of our petition comports with those warlike preparations which cover our waters and darken our land. Are fleets and armies necessary to a work of love and reconciliation? Have we shown ourselves so unwilling to be reconciled, that force must be called in to win back our love? Let us not deceive ourselves, sir. These are the implements of war and subjugation; the last arguments to which kings resort.

I ask gentlemen, sir, what means this martial array, if its purpose be not to force us to submission? Can gentlemen assign any other possible motive for it? Has Great Britain any enemy, in this quarter of the world, to call for all this accumulation of navies and armies? No, sir, she has none. They are meant for us: they can be meant for no other. They are sent over to bind and rivet upon us those chains, which the British ministry have been so long forging. And what have we to oppose them? Shall we try argument? Sir, we have been trying that for the last ten years. Have we anything new to offer upon the subject? Nothing. We have held the subject up in every light of which it is capable; but it has been all in vain.

Shall we resort to entreaty and humble supplication? What terms shall we find, which have not been already exhausted? Let us not, I beseech you, sir, deceive ourselves longer. Sir, we have done everything that could be done, to avert the storm which is now coming on. We have petitioned; we have remonstrated; we have supplicated; we have prostrated ourselves before the throne, and have implored its interposition to arrest the tyrannical hands of the ministry and parliament. Our petitions have been slighted; our remonstrances have produced additional violence and insult; our supplications have been disregarded; and we have been spurned, with contempt, from the foot of the throne!

In vain, after these things, may we indulge the fond hope of peace and reconciliation. There is no longer any room for hope. If we wish to be free,—if we mean to preserve inviolate those inestimable privileges, for which we have been so long contending,—if we mean not basely to abandon the noble struggle, in which we have been so long engages, and which we have pledged ourselves never to abandon, until the glorious object of our contest shall be obtained,—we must fight! I repeat it, sir, we must fight! An appeal to arms, and to the God of Hosts, is all that is left us!

They tell us, sir, that we are weak; unable to cope with so formidable an adversary. But when shall we be stronger? Will it be the next week, or the next year? Will it be when we are totally disarmed, and when a British guard shall be stationed in every house? Shall we gather strength by irresolution and inaction? Shall we acquire the means of effectual resistance, by lying supinely on our backs and hugging the delusive phantom of hope, until our enemies shall have bound us hand and foot? Sir, we are not weak, if we make a proper use of those means which the God of nature hath placed in our power.

Three millions of people, armed in the holy cause of liberty, and in such a country as that which we possess, are invincible by any force which our enemy can sent against us. Besides, sir, we shall not fight our battles alone. There is a just God who presides over the destinies of nations; and who will raise up friends to fight our battles for us. The battle, sir, is not to the strong alone; it is to the vigilant, the active, the brace. Besides, sir, we have no election (choice). If we were base enough to desire it, it is now too late to retire from the contest. There is no retreat, but in submission and slavery! Our chains are forged! Their clanking may be heard on the plans of Boston! The war is inevitable,— and let it come! I repeat it, sir, let it come!

It is in vain, sir, to extenuate the matter. Gentlemen may cry, peace, peace,--but there is no peace. The war is actually begun! The next gale, that sweeps from the north, will bring to our ears the clash of resounding arms! Our brethren are already in the field! Why stand we here idle? What is it that gentlemen wish? What would they have? Is life so dear, or peace so sweet, as to be purchased at the price of chains and slavery? Forbid it, Almighty God! I know not what course others may take; but as for me, give me liberty, or give me death!

LESSON 3:
DUTIES OF AMERICAN CITIZENS
—LEVI WOODBURY

It behooves us to look our perils and difficulties, such as they are, in the face. Then, with the exercise of candor, calmness, and fortitude, being able to comprehend fully their character and extent, let us profit by the teachings of almost every page in our annals, that any defects, under our existing system, have resulted more from the manner of administering it, then from its substance or form.

We less need new laws, new institutions, or new powers, than we need, on all occasions, at all times, and in all places, the requisite intelligence concerning the true spirit of our present ones; the high moral courage, under every hazard, and against every offender, to execute with fidelity the authority already possessed; and the manly independence to abandon all supineness, irresolution, vacillation, and time-serving pusillanimity, and enforce our present mild system with that uniformity and steady vigor throughout, which alone can supply the place of the greater severity of less free institutions.

To arm and encourage us in renewed efforts to accomplish everything on this subject which is desirable, our history constantly points her finger to a most efficient resource, and indeed to the only elixir, to secure a long life to any popular government, in increased attention to useful education and sound morals, with the wise description of equal measures and just practices they inculcate on every leaf of recorded time. Before their alliance, the spirit of misrule will always, in time, stand rebuked, and those who worship at the shrine of unhallowed ambition, must quail.

Storms, in the political atmosphere, may occasionally happen by the encroachments of usurpers, the corruption or intrigues of demagogues, or in the expiring agonies of faction, or by the sudden fury of popular frenzy; but, with the restraints and salutary influences of the allies before described, these storms will purify as healthfully as they often do in the physical world, and cause the tree of liberty, instead of falling, to strike its roots deeper. In this struggle, the enlightened and moral possess also a power, auxiliary and strong, in the spirit of the age, which is not only with them, but onward, in everything to ameliorate or improve.

When the struggle assumes the form of a contest with power, in all its subtlety, or with undermining and corrupting wealth, as it sometimes may, rather than with turbulence, sedition, or open aggression by the needy and desperate, it will be indispensable to employ still greater diligence; to cherish earnestness of purpose, resoluteness in conduct; to apply hard and constant blows to real abuses, rather than milk-and-water remedies, and encourage not only bold, free, and original thinking, but determined action.

In such a cause, our fathers were men whose hearts were not accustomed to fail them, through fear, however formidable the obstacles.... We are not, it is trusted, cach degenerate descendants, as to prove recreant, and fail to defend, with gallantry and firmness as unflinching, all which we have either derived from them, or since added to the rich inheritance.

At such a crisis, therefore, and in such a cause, yielding to neither consternation nor despair, may we not all profit by the vehement exhortations of Cicero to Atticus: "If you are asleep, awake; if you are standing, move; if you are moving, run; if you are running, fly?"

All these considerations warn us,--the grave-stones of almost every former republic warn us,--that a high standard of moral rectitude, as well as of intelligence, is quite as indispensable to communities, in their public doings as to individuals, if they would escape from either degeneracy or disgrace.

LESSON 4:
MILITARY INSUBORDINATION
—HENRY CLAY

Mr. Chairman,—I trust that I shall be indulged with some few reflections upon the danger of permitting the conduct, on which it has been my painful duty to animadvert, to pass without a solemn expression of the disapprobation of this house. Recall to your recollection, sir, the free nations which have gone before us. Where are they now?

> "Gone glimmering through the dream of things that were,
> A schoolboy's tale, the wonder of an hour."

And how have they lost their liberties? If we could transport ourselves back, sir, to the ages, when Greece and Rome flourished in their greatest prosperity, and, mingling in the throng, should ask a Grecian, if he did not fear that some daring military chieftain, covered with glory, some Philip, or Alexander, would one day overthrow the liberties of his country,—the confident and indignant Grecian would exclaim, 'No! no! we have nothing to fear from our heroes; our liberties will be eternal.' If a Roman citizen had been asked, if he did not fear that the conqueror of Gaul might establish a throne upon the ruins of public liberty, he would have instantly repelled the unjust insinuation. Yet Greece has fallen; Caesar has passed the Rubicon;

and the patriotic arm even of Brutus could not preserve the liberties of his devoted country.

Sir, we are fighting a great moral battle, for the benefit, not only of our country, but of all mankind. The eyes of the whole world are in fixed attention upon us. One, and the largest portion of it, is gazing with jealousy, and with envy; the other portion, with hope, with confidence, and with affection. Everywhere, the black cloud of legitimacy, is suspended over the world, save only one bright spot, which breaks out from the political hemisphere of the west, to enlighten, and animate, and gladden, the human heart. Obscure that, by the downfall of liberty here, and all mankind are enshrouded in a pall of universal darkness. Beware, then, sir, how you give a fatal sanction, in this infant period of our republic, to military insubordination. Remember that Greece had her Alexander, Rome her Caesar, England her Cromwell, France her Bonaparte; and, that if we would escape the rock on which they split, we must avoid their errors.

I hope, sir, that gentlemen will deliberately survey the awful isthmus, on which we stand. They may bear down all opposition. They may even vote the general (General Jackson) the public thanks. They may carry him triumphantly through this house. But if they do, sir, in my humble judgment, it will be a triumph of the principle of insubordination,—a triumph of the military over the civil authority,—a triumph over the powers of this house,—a triumph over the constitution of the land,—and I pray, sir, most devoutly, that it may not prove, in its ultimate effects and consequences, a triumph over the liberties of the people.

LESSON 5:
POLITICAL CORRUPTION
—GEO. M'DUFFIE

S ir,—we are apt to treat the idea of our own corruptibility, as utterly visionary, and to ask, with a grave affectation of dignity,—what! Do you think a member of congress can be corrupted? Sir, I speak what I have long and deliberately considered, when I say, that since man was created, there never has been a political body on the face of the earth, that would not be corrupted under the same circumstances. Corruption steals upon us, in a thousand insidious forms, when we are least aware of its approaches.

Of all the forms in which it can present itself, the bribery of office is the most dangerous, because it assumes the guise of patriotism to accomplish its fatal sorcery. We are often asked, where is the evidence of corruption? Have you seen it? Sir, do you expect to see it? You might as well expect to see the embodied forms of pestilence and famine stalking before you, as to see the latent operations of this insidious power. We may walk amidst it, and breathe its contagion, without being conscious of its presence. All experience teaches us the irresistible power of temptation, when vice assumes the form of virtue.

The great enemy of mankind could not have consummated his infernal scheme for the seduction of our first parents, but for the disguise in which he presented himself. Had he appeared, as the devil, in his proper form; had the spear of Ithuriel disclosed the naked deformity of the fiend of hell, the inhabitants of Paradise would have shrunk, with horror, from his presence. But he came, as the insinuating serpent, and presented a beautiful apple, the most delicious fruit in all the garden. He told his glowing story, to the unsuspecting victim of his guile. "It can be no crime to taste of this delightful fruit. It will disclose to you the knowledge of good and evil. It will raise you to an equality with the angels." Such, sir, was the process; and, in this simple but impressive narrative, we have the most beautiful and philosophical illustration of the frailty of man, and the power of temptation, that could possibly be exhibited.

Mr. Chairman, I have been forcibly struck with the similarity between our present situation and that of Eve, after it was announced that Satan was on the borders of Paradise. We, too, have been warned that the enemy is on our borders. But God forbid that the similitude should be carried any farther. Eve, conscious of her innocence, sought temptation, and defied it. The catastrophe is too fatally known to us all. She went, "with the blessings of Heaven on her head, and its purity in her heart," guarded by the ministry of angels,—she returned, covered with shame, under the heavy denunciation of Heaven's everlasting curse.

Sir, it is innocence that temptation conquers. If our first parent, pure as she came from the hand of God, was overcome by the seductive power, let us not imitate her fatal rashness, seeking temptation, when it is in our power to avoid it. Let us not vainly confide in our own infallibility. We are liable to be corrupted. To an ambitious man, an honorable office will appear as beautiful and fascinating, as the apple of Paradise.

I admit, sir, that ambition is a passion, at once the most powerful and the most useful. Without it, human affairs would become a mere stagnant pool. By means of his patronage, the president addresses himself, in the most irresistible manner, to this, the noblest and strongest of our passions. All that the imagination can desire,—honor, power, wealth, ease,—Satan himself could not devise,—a system which would more infallibly introduce corruption and death, into our political Eden. Sir, the angels fell from heaven, with less temptation.

LESSON 6:

INTELLIGENCE NECESSARY
TO PERPETUATE INDEPENDENCE—DAWES

That education is one of the deepest principles of independence, need not be labored in this assembly. In arbitrary governments, where the people neither make the law, nor choose those who legislate, the more ignorance, the more peace. But in a government, where the people fill all the branches of the sovereignty, intelligence is the life of liberty. An American would resent his being denied the use of his musket; but he would deprive himself of a stronger safeguard, if he should want that learning which is necessary to a knowledge of the constitution. It is easy to see, that our Agrarian law, and the law of education, were calculated to make republicans, to make men. Servitude could never long consist with the habits of such citizens. Enlightened minds, and virtuous manners, lead to the gates of glory.

The sentiment of independence must have been connatural in the bosoms of Americans; and, sooner or later, must have blazed out, into public action. Independence fits the soul of her residence, for every noble enterprise of humanity and greatness. Her radiant smile lights up celestial ardor in poets and orators, who sound her praises through all ages; in legislators and philosophers, who fabricate wise and happy governments, as dedications to her fame; in patriots and heroes, who shed their lives in sacrifice to her divinity. At this idea, do not our minds swell with the memory of those, whose godlike virtues have founded her most magnificent temple in America? It is easy for us to maintain her doctrines, at this late day, when there is but one party, on the subject, an immense people.

But what tribute shall we bestow, what sacred paean shall we raise over the tombs of those who dared, in the face of unrivalled power, and within the reach of majesty, to blow the blast of freedom throughout a subject continent? Nor did those brave countrymen of ours only express the emotions of glory; the nature of their principles inspired them with the power of practice, and they offered their bosoms to the shafts of battle. Bunker's awful mount is the capacious urn of their ashes; but the flaming bounds of the universe could not limit the flight of their minds. They fled to the union of kindred souls; and those who fell at the strait of Thermophylae, and those who bled on the heights of Charlestown, now reap congenial joys, in the fields of the blessed.

LESSON 7:
EXCELLENCE OF THE HOLY SCRIPTURES
—BEATTIE

Is it bigotry to believe the sublime truths of the Gospel, with full assurance of faith? I glory in such bigotry. I would not part with it for a thousand worlds. I congratulate the man who is possessed of it: for, amidst all the vicissitudes and calamities of the present state, that man enjoys an inexhaustible fund of consolation, of which it is not in the power of fortune to deprive him.

There is not a book on earth, so favorable to all the kind, and all the sublime affections; or so unfriendly to hatred and persecution, to tyranny, to injustice, and every sort of malevolence, as the Gospel. It breathes nothing throughout, but mercy, benevolence, and peace.

Poetry is sublime, when it awakens in the mind any great and good affection, as piety or patriotism. This is one of the noblest effects of the art. The Psalms are remarkable, beyond all other writings, for their power of inspiring devout emotions. But it is not in this respect only, that they are sublime. Of the divine nature, they contain the most magnificent descriptions, that the soul of man can comprehend. The hundred and fourth Psalm, in particular, displays the power and goodness of Providence, in creating and preserving the world, and the various tribes of animals in it, with such majestic brevity and beauty, as it is vain to look for any human composition.

Such of the doctrines of the Gospel, as are level to human capacity, appear to be agreeable to the purest truth, and the soundest morality. All the genius and learning of the heathen world, all the penetration of Pythagoras, Socrates, and Aristotle, had never been able to produce such a system of moral duty, and so rational an account of Providence and of man, as are to be found in the New Testament. Compared, indeed, with this, all other moral and theological wisdom

Loses, discountenanced, and like folly shows.

LESSON 8:

SPEECH OF MR. GRIFFIN
AGAINST CHEETHAM

I am one of those who believe, that the heart of the willful and the deliberate libeler, is blacker than that of the highway robber, or of one who commits the crime of midnight arson. The man, who plunders on the highway, may have the semblance of an apology for what he does. An affectionate wife may demand subsistence; a circle of helpless children raise to him the supplicating hand for food. He may be driven to the desperate act, by the high mandate of imperative necessity. The mild features of the husband and the father, may intermingle with those of the robber, and soften the roughness of the shade. But the robber of character plunders that which "not enricheth him," though it makes his neighbor "poor indeed."

The man who, at the midnight hour, consumes his neighbor's dwelling, does him an injury which perhaps is not irreparable. Industry may rear another habitation. The storm may indeed descend upon him, until charity opens a neighboring door: the rude winds of heaven may whistle around his uncovered family. But he looks forward to better days; he has yet a hook to hang a hope on.

No such consolation cheers the heart of him whose character has been torn from him. If innocent, he may look, like Anaxagoras, to the heavens; but he must be constrained to feel, that his world is to him a wilderness. For whither shall he go? Shall he dedicate himself to the service of his country? But will his country receive him? Will she employ in her councils, or in her armies, the man at whom the "slow, unmoving finger of scorn" is pointed? Shall he betake himself to the fire-side? The story of his disgrace will enter his own doors before him. And can he hear, think you, can he bear the sympathizing agonies of a distressed wife? Can he endure the formidable presence of scrutinizing, sneering domestics? Will his children receive instruction for the lips of a disgraced father?

Gentlemen, I am not ranging on fairy ground. I am telling the plain story of my client's wrongs. By the ruthless hand of malice, his character has been wantonly massacred;—and he now appears before a jury of his country for redress. Will you deny him this redress?—Is character valuable? On this point I will not insult you with argument. There are certain things, to argue which is treason against nature. The Author of our being did not intend to leave this point afloat at the mercy of opinion; but, with his own hand, has he kindly planted in the soul of man an instinctive *love of character.*

This high sentiment has no affinity to pride. It is the ennobling quality of the soul: and if we have hitherto ben elevated above the ranks of surrounding creation, human nature owes its elevation to the *love of character.* It is the *love of character* for which the poet has

30

sung, the philosopher toiled, the hero bled. It is the *love of character* which wrought miracles at ancient Greece; the *love of character* is the eagle on which Rome rose to empire. And it is the *love of character* animating the bosom of her sons, on which America must depend in those approaching crises that may "try men's souls." Will a jury weaken this our nation's hope? Will they by their verdict pronounce to the youth of our country, that character is scarce worth possessing?

We read of that philosophy which can smile over the destruction of property,—of that religion which enables its possessor to extend the benign look of forgiveness and complacency, to his murderers. But it is not in the soul of man to bear the laceration of slander....

LESSON 9:

RECTITUDE OF CHARACTER —WILLIAM WIRT

The man who is so conscious of the rectitude of his intentions, as to be willing to open his bosom to the inspection of the world, is in possession of one of the strongest pillars of a decided character. The course of such a man will be firm and steady, because he has nothing to fear from the world, and is sure of the approbation and support of Heaven. While he, who is conscious of secret and dark designs, which, if known, would blast him, is perpetually shrinking and dodging from public observation, and is afraid of all around, and much more of all above him.

Such a man may, indeed, pursue his iniquitous plans steadily; he may waste himself to a skeleton in the guilty pursuit; but it is impossible that he can pursue them with the same health-inspiring confidence, and exulting alacrity, with him who feels, at every step, that he is in pursuit of honest ends, by honest means.

The clear, unclouded brow, the open countenance, the brilliant eye which can look an honest man steadfastly, yet courteously, in the face, the healthfully beating heart, and the firm, elastic step, belong to him whose bosom is free from guile, and who knows that all his motives and purposes are pure and right. Why should such a man falter in his course? He may be slandered; he may be deserted by the world; but he has that within which will keep him erect, and enable him to move onward in his course, with his eyes fixed on Heaven, which he knows will not desert him.

Let your first step, then, in that discipline which is to give you decision of character, be the heroic determination to be honest men, and to preserve this character through every vicissitude of fortune, and in every relation which connects you with society. I do not use this phrase, "honest men," in the narrow sense, merely, of meeting your pecuniary engagements, and paying your debts; for this the common pride of gentlemen will constrain you to do.

I use it in its larger sense of discharging all your duties, both public and private, both open and secret, with the most scrupulous, Heaven-attesting integrity: in that sense, farther, which drives from the bosom all little, dark, crooked, sordid, debasing considerations of self, and substitutes in their place a bolder, loftier, and nobler spirit: one that will dispose you to consider yourselves as born, not so much for yourselves, as for your country, and your fellow-creatures, and which will lead you to act, on every occasion, sincerely, justly, generously, magnanimously.

There is a morality on a larger scale, perfectly consistent with a just attention to your own affairs, which it would be the height of folly to neglect; a generous expansion, a proud elevation, and conscious greatness of character, which is the best preparation for a decided course, in every situation into which you can be thrown; and, it is to this high and noble tone of character that I would have you aspire.

I would not have you to resemble those weak and meagre streamlets, which lose their direction at every petty impediment that presents itself, and stop, and turn back, and creep around, and search out every little channel through which they may wind their feeble and sickly course. Nor yet would I have you to resemble the headlong torrent that carries havoc in its mad career.

But I would have you like the ocean, that noblest emblem of majestic Decision, which, in the calmest hour, still heaves its resistless might of waters to the shore, filling the heavens, day and night, with the echoes of its sublime Declaration of Independence, and tossing an sporting on its bed, with an imperial consciousness of strength that laughs at opposition. It is this depth, and weight, and power, and purity of character, that I would have you to resemble; and I would have you, like the waters of the ocean, to become the purer by your own action.

LESSON 10:
THE CHRISTIAN CHARACTER—E. COOPER

The true Christian must show that he is in earnest about religion. In the management of his worldly affairs, he must let it clearly be seen, that he is not influenced by a worldly mind; that his heart is not upon earth; that he pursues his worldly calling from a principle of DUTY, not from the sordid love of gain; and that, in truth, his treasures are in HEAVEN. He must, therefore, not only "provide things honest in the sight of all men;" not only avoid everything which is fraudulent and unjust in his dealings with others; not only openly protest against those iniquitous practices which the custom of trade too frequently countenances and approves;--but, also, he must let his moderation be known unto all men."

He must not push his gains with seeming eagerness, even to the utmost LAWFUL extent. He must exercise forbearance. He must be content with moderate profits. He must sometimes even forego advantages, which, in themselves, he might innocently take, lest he should seem to give any ground for suspecting that his heart is secretly set upon these things.

Thus, also, with respect to worldly pleasures; he must endeavor to convince men that the pleasures which RELIGION furnishes, are far greater than those which the world can yield. While, therefore, he conscientiously keeps from joining in those trifling, and, too often, profane amusements, in which ungodly men profess to seek their happiness, he must yet labor to show, that, in keeping from those things, he is, in respect to real happiness, no loser, but even a GAINER by religion. He must avoid everything which may look like moroseness and gloom. He must cultivate a cheerfulness of spirit. He must endeavor to show, in his whole deportment, the contentment and tranquility which naturally flow from heavenly affections, from a mind at peace with God, and from a hope full of IMMORTALITY.

The spirit which Christianity enjoins and produces, is so widely different from the spirit of the world, and so immensely superior to it, that, as it cannot fail of being noticed, so it cannot fail of being admired, even by those who are strangers to its power. Do you ask in what particulars this spirit shows itself? I answer, in the exercise of humility, of meekness, of gentleness; in a patient bearing of injuries; in a readiness to forgive offences; in a uniform endeavor to overcome evil with good; in self-denial and disinterestedness; in universal kindness and courtesy; in slowness to wrath; in an unwillingness to hear or to speak evil of others; in a forwardness to defend, to advise, and to assist them; in loving our enemies; in blessing them that curse us; in doing good to them that hate us. These are genuine fruits of true Christianity.

The Christian must "let his light shine before men," by discharging in a faithful, a diligent, and a consistent manner, the personal particular duties of his station.

As a member of society, he must be distinguished by a blameless and an inoffensive conduct; by a simplicity and an ingenuousness of character, free from every degree of guile; by uprightness and fidelity in all his engagements.

As a neighbor, he must be kind, friendly, and accommodating. His discourse must be mild and instructive. He must labor to prevent quarrels, to reconcile those who differ, to comfort the afflicted. In short, he must be "ready for every good work;" and all his dealing with others must show the HEAVENLY PRINCIPLE, which dwells and works in his HEART.

LESSON 11:
POPULAR GOVERNMENT
—DR. SHARP

The real glory and prosperity of a nation does not consist in the hereditary rank or titled privileges of a very small class in the community; in the great wealth of the few, and the great poverty of the many; in the splendid palaces of nobles, and the wretched huts of a numerous and half-famished peasantry. No! such a state of things may give pleasure to proud, ambitious, and selfish minds, but there is nothing here on which the eye of a patriot can rest with unmingled satisfaction. In his deliberate judgment,

> *"Ill fares the land, to hastening ills a prey,*
> *Where wealth accumulates, and men decay;*
> *Princes and lords may flourish or may fade;*
> *A breath can make them, as a breath has made:*
> *But a bold peasantry, their country's pride,*
> *When once destroyed, can never be supplied."*

It is an intelligent, virtuous, free, and extensive population, able, by their talents and industry, to obtain a competent support, which constitutes the strength and prosperity of a nation.

It is not the least advantage of a popular government, that it brings into operation a greater amount of talent than any other. It is acknowledged by everyone, that the occurrence of great events awakens the dormant energies of the human mind, and calls for the most splendid and powerful abilities. It was the momentous question, whether your country should be free and independent, and the declaration that it was so, which gave to you orators, statesmen, and generals, whose names all future ages will delight to honor.

The characters of men are generally molded by the circumstances in which they are placed. They seldom put forth their strength, without some powerfully exciting motives. But what motives can they have to qualify themselves for stations, from which they are forever excluded on account of plebeian extraction? How can they be expected to prepare themselves for the service of their country, when they know that their services would be rejected, because, unfortunately, they dissent from the established religion, and have honesty to avow it!

But in a country like ours, where the most obscure individuals in society may, by their talents, virtues, and public services, rise to the most honorable distinctions, and attain to the highest offices which the people can give, the most effectual inducements are presented. It is indeed true, that only a few who run in the race for political honor, can obtain the prize. But, although many come short, yet the exertions and the progress which they make, are not lost either on themselves or society. The suitableness of their talents and characters for some other important station, may have been perceived; at least the cultivation of their minds, and the effort to acquire an honorable reputation, may render them active and useful members of the community. These are some of the benefits peculiar to a popular government; benefits which we have long enjoyed.

LESSON 12:
REVERENCE FOR LAW
—J. HOPKINSON

Happy is that country and only that, where the laws are not only just and equal, but supreme and irresistible;—where selfish interests and disorderly passions are curbed by an arm to which they must submit.—We look back with horror and affright to the dark and troubled ages, when a cruel and gloomy superstition tyrannized over the people of Europe; dreaded alike by kings and people; by governments and individuals; before which the law had no force; justice no respect; and mercy no influence. The sublime precepts of morality, the kind and endearing charities; the true and rational reverence for a bountiful Creator, which are the elements and the life of our religion, were trampled upon in the reckless career of ambition, pride, and the lust of power. Nor was it much better when the arm of the warrior, and the sharpness of his sword, determined every question of right; and held the weak in bondage to the strong; and the revengeful feuds of the great, involved, in one common ruin, themselves and their humblest vassals.—These disastrous days are gone, never to return. There is no power but the law which is the power of all; and those who administer it are the masters and the ministers of all.

LESSON 13:
OUR DUTIES TO OUR COUNTRY
—DANIEL WEBSTER

This lovely land, this glorious liberty, these benign institutions, the dear purchase of our fathers, are ours; ours to enjoy, ours to preserve, ours to transmit. Generations past, and generations to come, hold us responsible for this sacred trust. Our fathers, from behind, admonish us, with their anxious paternal voices; posterity calls out to us, from the boom of the future; the world turns hither its solicitous eyes,—all, all conjure us to act wisely, and faithfully, in the relation which we sustain. We can never, indeed, pay the debt which is upon us; but by virtue, by morality, by religion, by the cultivation of every good principle and every good habit, we may hope to enjoy the blessing, through our day, and to leave it unimpaired to our children. Let us feel deeply how much, of what we are and what we possess, we owe to this liberty, and these institutions of government.

Nature has, indeed, given us a soil which yields bounteously to the hands of industry; the mighty and fruitful ocean is before us, and the skies over our heads shed health and vigor. But what are lands, and seas, and skies, to civilized men, without society, without knowledge, without morals, without religious culture? And how can these be enjoyed, in all their extent, and all their excellence, but under the protection of wise institutions and a free government?

Fellow-citizens, there is not one of us, there is not one of us here present, who does not, at this moment, and at every moment, experience in his own condition, and in the condition of those most near and dear to him, the influence and the benefits of this liberty, and these institutions. Let us then acknowledge the blessing; let us feel it deeply and powerfully; let us cherish a strong affection for it, and resolve to maintain and perpetuate it. The blood of our fathers, let it not have been shed in vain; the great hope of posterity, let it not be blasted.

The striking attitude, too, in which we stand to the world around us,--a topic to which, I fear, I advert too often, and dwell on too long,--cannot be altogether omitted here. Neither individuals nor nations can perform their part well, until they understand and feel its importance, and comprehend and justly appreciate all the duties belonging to it. It is not to inflate national vanity, nor to swell a light and empty feeling of self-importance; but it is that we may judge justly of our situation, and of our own duties, that I earnestly urge this consideration of our position, and our character among the nations of the earth.

It cannot be denied, but by those who would dispute against the sun, that with America, and in America, a new era commences in human affairs. This era is distinguished by free representative government, by entire religious liberty, by improved systems of national intercourse, by a newly awakened and an unconquerable spirit of free inquiry, and by a diffusion of knowledge through the community, much as has been before altogether unknown and unheard of. America, America, our country, our own dear and native land, is inseparably connected, fast bound up, in fortune and by fate, with these great interests. If they fall, we fall with them; if they stand, it will be because we have upheld them.

Let us contemplate, then, this connection which binds the prosperity of others to our own; and let us manfully discharge all the duties which it imposes. If we cherish the virtues and the principles of our fathers, Heaven will assist us to carry on the work of human liberty and human happiness. Auspicious omens cheer us. Great examples are before us. Our own firmament now shines brightly upon our path. Washington is in the clear upper sky. Those other stars have now joined the American constellation; they circle round their center, and the heavens beam with new light. Beneath this illumination, let us walk the course of life, and at its close devoutly commend our beloved country, the common parent of us all, to the Divine Benignity.

LESSON 14:

MEMORIALS OF
WHASHINGTON AND FRANKLIN
—JOHN QUINCY ADAMS

*(From Mr. Adams' speech on the reception,
by Congress, of the battle sword of Washington,
and the staff of Franklin.)*

The sword of Washington! The staff of Franklin! Oh! Sir, what associations are linked in adamant with these names! Washington, whose sword, as my friend (Geo. W. Summers) has said, was never drawn but in the cause of his country, and never sheathed when wielded in his country's cause! Franklin, the philosopher of the thunderbolt, the printing-press, and the plough-share!—What names are these in the scanty catalogue of the benefactors of human kind!

Washington and Franklin! What other two men, whose lives belong to the eighteenth century of Christendom, have left a deeper impression of themselves upon the age in which they lived, and upon all after time?

Washington, the warrior and the legislator! In war, contending, by the wager of battle, for the independence of his country, and for the freedom of the human race; ever manifesting, amidst its horrors, by

45

precept and example, his reverence for the laws of peace, and for the tenderest sympathies of humanity; in peace, soothing the ferocious spirit of discord, among his own countrymen, into harmony and union; and giving to that very sword, now presented to his country, a charm more potent than that attributed, in ancient times, to the lyre of Orpheus.

Franklin!—The mechanic of his own fortune; teaching, in early youth, under the shackles of indigence, the way to wealth, and in the shade of obscurity, the path to greatness; in the maturity of manhood, disarming the thunder of its terror, the lightning of its fatal blast; and wrestling from the tyrant's hand the still more effective scepter of oppression: while descending into the vale of years, traversing the Atlantic ocean, braving, in the dead of winter, the battle and the breeze, bearing in his hand the charter of Independence, which he had contributed to form, and tendering, from the self-created nation, to the mightiest monarchs of Europe, the olive-branch of peace, the mercurial wand of commerce, and the amulet of protection and safety to the man of peace, on the pathless ocean, from the inexorable cruelty and merciless rapacity of war.

And, finally, in the last stage of life, with fourscore winters upon his head, under the torture of an incurable disease, returning to his native land, closing his days as the chief magistrate of his adopted commonwealth, after contributing by his counsels, under the presidency of Washington, and recording his name, under the sanction of devout prayer, invoked by him to God, to that Constitution under the authority of which we are here assembled, as the representatives of the North American people, to receive, in their name and for them, these venerable relics of the wise, the valiant, and the good founders of our great confederated republic,—these sacred symbols of our golden age. May they be deposited among the archives of our government! And every American, who shall hereafter behold them, (speak forth) a mingled offering of praise to that Supreme Ruler of the Universe, by whose tender mercies our Union has been hitherto preserved, through all the vicissitudes and revolutions of this turbulent world,—and of prayer for the continuance of these blessings, by the dispensations of Providence, to our beloved country, from age to age, till time shall be no more!

LESSON 15:

THE LOVE OF TRUTH
—GEORGE PUTNAM

Truth is the one legitimate object of all intellectual endeavor. To discover and apprehend truth, to clear up and adorn it, to establish, and present, and commend it,—these are the processes and the ends of study and literature. To discern the things that really are, and how they are, to distinguish reality from appearance and sham, to know and declare the true in outward nature, in past time, in the results of speculation, in consciousness and sentiment,—this is the business of educated mind. Logic and the mathematics are instruments for this purpose, and so is the imagination just as strictly. A poem, a play, a novel, though a work of fiction, must be true, or it is a failure. Its machinery may be unknown to the actual world; the scene may be laid in Elysian fields, or infernal shades, or fairy land; but the law of truth must preside over the work; it must be the vehicle of truth, or it is naught, and is disallowed. The Tempest, the Odyssey, and Paradise Lost, derive their value from their truth; and I say this, not upon utilitarian principles, but according to the verdict which every true soul passes upon them, consciously or unconsciously. Lofty, holy truth, made beautiful and dear and winning to the responsive heart,— this is their charm, their wealth, their immortality. There is no permanent intellectual success but in truth attained and brought home to the eye, the understanding, or the heart.

And for the best success in the pursuit of any object, there must be a love of the object itself. The student, the thinker, the author, who is true to his vocation, loves the truth which he would develop and embody. Not for bread, not for fame, primarily, he works. These things may come, and are welcome; but truth is higher and dearer than these. Great things have been done for bread and fame, but not the greatest. Plato, pacing the silent groves of the academy, and Newton, sitting half a day on his bedside, undressed, and his fast unbroken, rapt in a problem of fluxions; Dante solacing the bitterness of exile with the meditations that live in the Commedia, and Bacon taking his death chill in an experiment to test the preserving qualities of snow; Cuvier a lordlier Adam than he of Eden, naming the whole animal world in his museum, and reading the very thoughts of God after him in their wondrous mechanism; Franklin and Davy wresting the secrets of nature from their inmost hiding-place; Linnaeus studying the flora of the arctic circle *in loco*; and that fresh old man who startles the clefts of the Rocky Mountains with his rifle, to catch precisely the lustrous tints of beauty in the plumage of a bird;—these men, and such as they, love truth, and are consecrate, hand and heart, to her service. The truth, as she stands in God's doings, or in man's doings, or in those thoughts and affections that have neither form nor speech, but which answer from the deep places of the soul,—truth, as seen in her sublimities or her beauties, in her world-poising might or her seeming trivialities,—truth, as she walks the earth embodied in visible facts, or moves among the spheres in the mysterious laws that combine a universe and spell it to harmony, or as she sings in the upper heavens the inarticulate wisdom which only a profound religion in the soul can interpret,—truth, in whichever of her myriad manifestations, she has laid hold of their noble affinities, and brought their being into holy captivity;—such men have loved her greatly and fondly; the soul of genius is always pledged to her in a single-hearted and sweet affiance, or else it is genius baffled, blasted, and dis-crowned.

PART II:
SELECTED LESSONS FROM

Gregg & Elliot's New Series
of Common School Readers, No. III, Chapter 3,
Abridgment of Seneca's Morals.

Philadelphia:
Grigg & Elliot, 1845.

*He that would know all things, let him read Seneca; the
most lively describer of public vices and manners, and
the smartest critic of them.—Lactantius*

*Next to the gospel itself, I do look upon Seneca's Morals,
as the most sovereign remedy against the miseries of
human nature. —L'Estrange*

LESSON 1:
ABRIDGMENT OF SENECA'S
DISCOURSE ON BENEFICENCE

An obstinate goodness overcomes an ill disposition, as a barren soil is made fruitful by care and tillage. But let a man be never so ungrateful or inhuman, he shall never destroy the satisfaction of my having done a good office.

But what if others will be wicked? Does it follow that we must be so too? If others will be ungrateful, must we therefore be inhuman? To give and to lose, is nothing; but to lose and to give still, is the part of a great mind. And the other's in effect, is the greater loss; for the one does but lose his benefit, and the other loses himself. The light shines upon the profane and sacrilegious as well as upon the righteous. The mariner puts to sea again after a wreck.

An illustrious mind does not propose the profit of a good office, but the duty. If the world be wicked, we should yet persevere in well-doing, even among evil men. I had rather never receive a kindness than never bestow one: not to return a benefit is the greater sin, but not to confer it is the earlier.

We cannot propose to ourselves a more glorious example than that of the Almighty, who neither needs nor expects anything from us;

and yet he is continually showering down and distributing his mercies and his grace among us, not only for our necessities, but also for our delights; as fruits and seasons, rain and sunshine, veins of water and of metal; and all this to the wicked as well as to the good, and without any other end than the common benefit of the receivers.

With what face then can we be mercenary one to another, that have received all things from Divine Providence *gratis*? It is a common saying, "I gave such or such a man so much money, I would I had thrown it into the sea:" and yet the merchant trades again after a piracy, and the banker ventures afresh after a bad security.

He that will do no good offices after a disappointment, must stand still, and do just nothing at all. The plow goes on after a barren year: and while the ashes are yet warm, we raise a new house upon the ruins of a former.

What obligations can be greater than those which children receive from their parents? And yet should we give them over in their infancy, it were all to no purpose. Benefits, like grain, must be followed from the seed to the harvest. I will not so much as leave any place for ingratitude. I will pursue, and I will encompass the receiver with benefits; so that let him look which way he will, his benefactor shall be still in his eye, even when he would avoid his own memory.

In a matter of money, it is a common thing to pay a debt out of course, and before it be due; but we account ourselves to owe nothing for a good office; whereas the benefit increases by delay. So insensible are we of the most important affair of human life.

That man were doubtless in a miserable condition, that could neither see, nor hear, nor taste, nor feel, nor smell: but much more unhappy is he than that, wanting a sense of benefits, loses the greatest comfort in nature in the bliss of giving and receiving them. He that takes a benefit as it is meant, is in the right; for the benefactor has then his end, and his only end, when the receiver is grateful.

LESSON 2:
ON A HAPPY LIFE, AND WHEREIN IT CONSISTS

There is not anything in this world, perhaps, that is more talked of, and less understood, than the business of a happy life. It is every man's wish and design; and yet not one of a thousand that knows wherein that happiness consists. We live, however, in a blind and eager pursuit of it; and the more haste we make in a wrong way, the farther we are from our journey's end.

Let us therefore, first, consider "what it is we should be at;" and secondly, "which is the readiest way to compass it." If we be right, we shall find every day how much we improve; but if we either follow the cry, or the track, of people that are out of the way, we must expect to be misled, and to continue our days in wandering and error.

Wherefore, it highly concerns us to take along with us a skillful guide; for it is not in this, as in other voyages, where the highway brings us to our place of repose, or it a man should happen to be out, where the inhabitants might set him right again; but on the contrary, the beaten road is here the most dangerous, and the people instead of helping us, misguide us. Let us not therefore follow, like beasts, but rather govern ourselves by reason, than by example.

It fares with us in human life as in a routed army; one stumbles first, and then another falls upon him, and so they follow, one upon the neck of another, until the whole field comes to be but on heap of miscarriages.

And the mischief is, "that the number of the multitude carries it against truth and justice;" so that we must leave the crowd if we would be happy: for the question of a happy life is not to be decided by vote: nay, so far from it, that plurality of voices is still an argument of the wrong; the common people find it easier to believe than to judge, and content themselves with what is usual, never examining whether it be good or not.

By the *common people* is intended the man of title as well as the clouted shoe: for I do not distinguish them by the eye, but by the mind, which is the proper judge of the man.

The true felicity of life is to be free from perturbations; to understand our duties toward God and man: to enjoy the present without any anxious dependence upon the future. The great blessings of mankind are within us, and within our reach; but we shut our eyes, and, like people in the dark, we fall foul upon the very thing we search for without finding it.

"Tranquility is a certain equality of mind, which no condition of fortune can either exalt or depress." "True joy is a serene and sober motion;" and they are miserably out that take laughing for rejoicing. The seat of it is within, and there is no cheerfulness like the resolution of a brave mind, that has fortune under his feet. He that can look death in the face, and bid it welcome; open his door to poverty, and bridle his appetites; this is the man whom Providence has established in the possession of inviable delights. The pleasures of the vulgar are ungrounded, thin, and superficial; but the other are solid and eternal.

As the body itself is rather a necessary thing than a great; so the comforts of it are but temporary and vain; beside that, without extraordinary moderation, their end is only pain and repentance; whereas, a peaceful conscience, honest thoughts, virtuous actions, and an indifference for casual events, are blessings without end, satiety, or measure.

This consummated state of felicity is only a submission to the dictate of right nature; "The foundation of it is wisdom and virtue; the knowledge of what we ought to do, and the conformity of the will to that knowledge."

LESSON 3:

HUMAN HAPPINESS IS FOUNDED UPON WISDOM AND VIRTUE

Taking for granted that human happiness is founded upon wisdom and virtue, we shall treat of these two points in order as they lie; and, first, of wisdom; not in the latitude of its various operations, but as it has only a regard to a good life, and the happiness of mankind.

Wisdom is a right understanding, a faculty of discerning good from evil; what is to be chosen, and what rejected; a judgment grounded upon the value of things, and not the common opinion of them; an equality of force, and a strength of resolution. It sets a watch over our words and deeds, it takes us up with the contemplation of the works of nature, and makes us invincible to either good or evil fortune.

It is the habit of a perfect mind, and the perfection of humanity, raised as high as nature can carry it. It differs from philosophy, as avarice and money; the one desires, and the other is desired; the one is the effect and the reward of the other. To be wise is the use of wisdom, as seeing is the use of eyes, and well speaking the use of eloquence.

He that is perfectly wise is perfectly happy; nay the very beginning of wisdom makes life easy to us. Neither is it enough to know this, unless we print it in our minds by daily meditation, and so bring a good will to a good habit.

And we, must practice what we preach: for philosophy is not a subject for popular ostentation; nor does it rest in words, but in things. It is not an entertainment taken up for delight, or to give a taste to our leisure; but it fashions the mind, governs our actions, tells what we are to do, and what not.

It sits at the helm, and guides us through all hazards: nay, we cannot be safe without it, for every hour gives us occasion to make use of it. It informs us in all the duties of life, piety to our parents, faith to our friends, charity to the miserable, judgment in counsel; it gives us peace by fearing nothing, and riches by coveting nothing.

There is no condition of life that excludes a wise man from discharging his duty. If his fortune be good, he tempers it; if bad, he masters it; if he has an estate, he will exercise his virtue in plenty; if none, in poverty.

Some accidents there are, which I confess may affect him, but not overthrow him, as bodily pains, loss of children and friends; the ruin and desolation of a man's country. One must be made of stone, or iron, not to be sensible of these calamities: and beside, it were no virtue to bear them, if a body did not feel them. If there were nothing else in it, a man would apply himself to wisdom, because it settles him in a perpetual tranquility of mind.

LESSON 4:
THERE CAN BE NO HAPPINESS WITHOUT VIRTUE

Virtue is that perfect good, which is the complement of a happy life; the only immortal thing that belongs to mortality: it is the knowledge both of others and itself; it is an invincible greatness of mind not to be elevated or dejected with good or ill fortune.

It is sociable and gentle, free, steady, and fearless: content within itself; full of inexhaustible delights; and it is valued for itself. One may be a good physician, a good governor, a good grammarian, without being a good man; so that all things from without are only accessories: for the seat of it is a pure and holy mind.

It consists in a congruity of actions which we can never expect so long as we are distracted by our passions. It is not the matter, but the virtue, that makes the action good or ill; and he that is led in triumph may be yet greater than his conqueror.

When we come once to value our flesh above our honesty, we are lost; and yet I would not press upon dangers, no, not so much as upon inconveniences, unless where the man and the brute come in competition: and in such a case, rather than make a forfeiture of my credit, my reason, or my faith, I would run all extremities.

It is by an impression of nature that all men have a reverence for virtue; they know it, and they have a respect for it, though they do not practice it: nay, for the countenance of their very wickedness, they miscall it virtue. Their injuries they call benefits, and expect a man should thank them for doing him a mischief; they cover their most notorious iniquities with a pretext of justice.

He that robs upon the highway, had rather find his booty than force it. Ask any of them that live upon rapine, fraud, oppression, if they had not rather enjoy a fortune honestly gotten, and their consciences will not suffer them to deny it.

Men are vicious only for the profit of villainy; for, at the same time that they commit it, they condemn it. Nay, so powerful is virtue, and so gracious is Providence, that every man has a light set up within him for a guide; which we do all of us both see and acknowledge, though we do not pursue it. (See also Ovid, Metamorphoses, vii. 20, "I know the right, and I approve it too; condemn the wrong, and yet the wrong pursue".)

What I do shall be done for conscience, not ostentation. I will eat and drink, not to gratify my palate, but to satisfy nature: I will be cheerful to my friends, mild and open to being placated to my enemies: I will prevent an honest request, if I can foresee it, and I will grant it without asking: I will look upon the whole world as my country: I will live and die with this testimony, that I loved good studies and a good conscience; that I never invaded another man's liberty, and that I preserved my own.

Virtue is divided into two parts, contemplation and action. The one is delivered by institution, the other by admonition: one part of virtue consists in discipline; the other in exercise; for we must first learn, and then practice. The sooner we begin to apply ourselves to it, and the more haste we make, the longer shall we enjoy the comforts of a rectified mind; nay, we have the fruition of it in the very act of forming it: but it is another sort of delight, I must confess, that arises from the contemplation of a soul which is advanced into the possession of wisdom and virtue.

If it was so great a comfort to us to pass from the subjection of our childhood into a state of liberty and business, how much greater will it be when we come to cast off the boyish levity of our minds, and range ourselves among the philosophers?

We are past our minority, it is true, but not our indiscretion; and, which is yet worse, we have the authority of seniors, and the weaknesses of children, (I might have said of infants, for every little thing frights the one, and every trivial fancy the other.)

For virtue is open to all; as ell to servants and exiles, as to princes: it is profitable to the world and to itself, at all distances and in all conditions; and there is no difficulty that can excuse a man from the exercise of it.

Nay, the mind itself has its variety of perverse pleasures as well as the body; as insolence, self-conceit, pride, garrulity, laziness, and the abusive wit of turning everything into ridicule; whereas virtue weighs all this and corrects it.

LESSON 5:

THE DUE CONTEMPLATION OF DIVINE PROVIDENCE IS A REMEDY AGAINST ALL MISFORTUNE

Whoever observes the world, and the order of it, will find all the motions in it, to be only the vicissitudes of falling and rising; nothing extinguished, and even those things which seem to us to perish, are in truth but changed.

The seasons go and return, day and night follow in their courses, the heavens roll, and nature goes on with her work: all things succeed in their turns, storms and calms; the law of nature will have it so, which we must follow and obey, accounting all things that are done to be well done: so that what we cannot mend we must suffer, and wait upon Providence without repining.

It is the part of a cowardly soldier to follow his commander groaning; but a generous man delivers himself up to God without struggling; and it is only for a narrow mind to condemn the order of the world, and to propound rather the mending of nature than of himself.

In the very methods of nature we cannot but observe the regard that Providence had to the good of mankind, even in the disposition of the world, in providing so amply for our maintenance and satisfaction. It is not possible for us to comprehend what the Power is which has made all things; some few sparks of that Divinity are discovered, but infinitely the greater part of it lies hid. We are all of us, however, thus far agreed, first, in the acknowledgment and belief of that Almighty Being; and, secondly, that we are to ascribe to it all majesty and goodness.

Fabricius took more pleasure in eating the roots of his own planting than in all the delicacies of luxury and expense. Prudence and religion are above accidents, and draw god out of everything; affliction keeps a man in use, and makes him strong, patient, and hardy.

Providence treats us like a generous father, and brings us up to labors, toils, and dangers; whereas … indulgence … makes us weak and spiritless. No man can be happy that does not stand firm against all contingencies.

LESSON 6:

OF LEVITY OF MIND, AND
OTHER IMPEDIMENTS OF A HAPPY LIFE

Now, to sum up what is already delivered, we have showed what happiness is, and wherein it consists; that it is founded upon wisdom and virtue; for we must first know what we ought to do, and then live according to that knowledge.

We have also discoursed the helps of philosophy a precepts towards a happy life; the blessing of a good conscience; that a good man can never be miserable, nor a wicked many happy; nor any man unfortunate, that cheerfully submits to Providence. We shall now examine, how it comes to pass that, when the certain way to happiness lies so fair before us, men will yet steer their course on the other side, which as manifestly leads to ruin.

There are some who live without any design at all, and only pass in the world like straws upon a river; they do not go, but they are carried. Some there are that torment themselves afresh with the memory of what is past: "Lord! What did I endure? Never was any man in my condition; everybody gave me over; my very heart was ready to break," and etc.

Others, again, afflict themselves with the apprehension of evils to come; and very ridiculously both: for the one does not now concern us, and the other not yet: beside that, there may be remedies for mischiefs likely to happen.

Levity of mind is a great hindrance to repose; it is only philosophy that makes the mind invincible, and places us out of the reach of fortune, so that all her arrows fall short of us. This it is that reclaims the rage of our passions, and sweetens the anxiety of our fears.

Place me among princes or among beggars, the one shall not make me proud, nor the other ashamed. I can take as sound a sleep in a barn as in a palace, and a bundle of hay makes me as good a lodging as a bed of dawn. I will not transport myself with either pain or pleasure; but yet for all that, I could wish that I had an easier game to play, and that I were put rather to moderate my joys than my sorrows.

Never pronounce any man happy that depends upon fortune for his happiness; for nothing can be more preposterous than to place the good of a reasonable creature in unreasonable things. If I have lost anything, it was adventitious; and the less money, the less trouble; the less favor the less envy.

That which we call our own is but lent us; and what we have received *gratis* we must return without complaint. That which fortune gives us this hour, she may take away the next; and he that trusts to her favor, shall either find himself deceived, or it he be not, he will at least be troubled, because he may be so.

But the best of it is, if a man cannot men his fortune, he may yet mend his manners, and put himself so far out of her reach, that whether she gives or takes, it shall be all one to us; for we are neither the greater for the one, nor the less for the other.

LESSON 7:

ANGER IS A SHORT MADNESS;
AND A DEFORMED VICE

H e was much in the right, whoever it was, that first called anger a short madness; for they have both of them the same symptoms; and there is so wonderful a resemblance betwixt the transports of choler and those of frenzy, that it is a hard matter to know the one from the other.

A bold, fierce, and threatening countenance, as pale as ashes, and, in the same moment, as red as blood; a glaring eye, a wrinkled brow, violent motions, the hands restless and perpetually in action, wringing and menacing, snapping of the joints, stamping with the feet, the hair starting, trembling lips, a forced and squeaking voice; the speech false and broken, deep and frequent sighs, and ghastly looks; the veins swell, the heart pants, the knees knock; with a hundred dismal accidents that are common to both distempers.

Neither in anger a bare resemblance only of madness, but many times an irrevocable transition into the thing itself. How many persons have we known, read, and heard of, that have lost their wits in a passion, and never came to themselves again? It is therefore to be avoided, not only for moderation's sake, but also for health.

Now, if the outward appearance of anger be so foul and hideous, how deformed must that miserable mind be, that is harassed with it? For it leaves no place either for counsel or friendship, honesty or good manners; no place either for the exercise of reason, or for the offices of life.

If I were to describe it, I would draw a tiger bathed in blood, sharp teeth, and ready to take a leap at his prey; or dress it up as poets represent the furies, with whips, snakes, and flames; it should be sour, livid, full of scars, and wallowing in gore, raging up and down, destroying, grinning, bellowing, and pursuing; sick of all other things, and most of all itself. It turns beauty into deformity, and the calmest counsels into fierceness: it disorders our very garments, and fills the mind with horror.

How abominable is it in the soul then, when it appears so hideous even through the bones, the skin, and so many impediments? Is he not a madman that has lost the government of himself, and is tossed hither and thither by his fury, as by a tempest? The executioner and the murder of his nearest friends? The smallest matter moves it, and makes us unsociable and inaccessible. It does all things by violence, as well upon itself as others; and it is, in short, the master of all passions.

A vice that carries along with it neither pleasure nor profit, neither honor nor security; but on the contrary, destroys us to all the comfortable and glorious purposes of our reasonable being. Some there are, that will have the root of it to be the greatness of mind.

And, why may we not as well entitle impudence to courage, whereas the one is proud, the other brave; the one is gracious and gentle, the other rude and furious? At the same rate, we may ascribe magnanimity to avarice, luxury, and ambition, which are all but splendid impotences, without measure and without foundation.

There is nothing great but what is virtuous, nor indeed truly great, but what is also composed and quiet. Anger, alas, is but a wild impetuous blast, and empty tumor, the very infirmity of children; a brawling, clamorous evil: and the more noise the less courage; as we find it commonly, that the boldest tongues have the faintest hearts.

PART III:
EDITOR'S COMMENTARY REGARDING THE SIMILARITY OF SENECA'S WRITINGS TO THE TEACHINGS OF JESUS

WHY ARE THE WRITINGS OF SENECA SO VERY SIMILAR TO THE TEACHINGS OF CHRIST?

I think this is an important question. My own answer is based upon personal experience. I'm sharing it with you, dear reader, as it may help you in finding your own answer.

During my late high school years, I began keeping a journal of sorts, just random thoughts from time to time that struck me as being significant somehow. As the years passed, looking back upon what I had written, I realized that my thoughts were strikingly similar to some of the things I later discovered in Aristotle's Nicomachean Ethics, and, in the writings of Seneca. Now, it is important, I think, to emphasize that at the time I had written those journal entries I had not yet read the Nicomachean Ethics, nor was I at the time familiar with the writings of Seneca. What I had written, however, bore more than a passing semblance to many of the concepts advanced by both of those philosophers. When I discovered Aristotle's Ethics and the writings of Seneca, the impact was electrifying. I immediately understood that the thoughts I had recorded as a young man, while mine, were also somehow connected to a universal truth.

The point of sharing this with you, dear reader, is that I firmly believe that the Holy Spirit was at work in my heart and mind, bearing witness to a universal and timeless truth. I didn't invent the truth of the Nicomachean Ethics any more than Aristotle invented it. And Seneca didn't invent the truth to which he bore witness. Moreover, the teachings of Jesus are not true simply because he said them. He said them because they are true. Jesus bore witness to the truth (see John 18:37).

Others have proposed a different explanation to account for the striking similarities between what Seneca wrote and what Jesus, according to the gospels, taught. Their theory is that Seneca wrote a fictional play about Jesus prior to the appearance of the Gospels, and that the biblical accounts of the teachings of Jesus were fashioned after that fictional play. There are, in my opinion, more than sufficient arguments to test that accusation. Luke's statement in Luke 1:1-4, for example, tells us that prior to writing his account he carefully investigated the accounts of Jesus given by those who were eyewitnesses. It is not plausible that people would claim to be eyewitnesses if Jesus were a fictional character invented by Seneca. Moreover, no such play by Seneca has ever been found. Then there is the Apostle Paul who had once tried to stamp out Christianity but who, because of a personal encounter with the risen Christ, became a Christian who devoted the rest of his life to teaching and sharing the Gospel of Jesus Christ. I think textual analysis would also raise many objections to the suggestion that Seneca had perhaps introduced some sort of fictional "proto gospel" which was later developed by Matthew, Mark, Luke and John into the biblical accounts of the life and teachings of Jesus.

Moreover, because of my own personal experience, the experience that I have related it to you, dear reader, it seems perfectly clear to me that the teachings of Seneca simply foreshadowed the truths that would be taught by Jesus. My conclusion as to why the writings of Seneca seem so similar to the teachings of Jesus, is that the Holy Spirit was preparing the hearts and minds of the classical world through the philosophical teachings of Seneca (and Aristotle) for the Gospel of Jesus Christ.

In 313 AD, the Emperor Constantine issued the Edict of Milan, which accepted Christianity as a legal religion in the Empire. Ten years later, Christianity had become the official religion of the Roman Empire.

This could only have come about because God had been at work for centuries in the hearts and minds of the classical writers, including Seneca who was a contemporary of Jesus, preparing the Empire for acceptance of the Gospel of Jesus Christ.

—B. Perrine

PART IV:
SELECTED LESSONS FROM

The Pleasing Instructor, or
Entertaining Moralist by Anne Fisher

Boston:
Printed by Joseph Bumstead, 1795)

Note:
Fisher was an English grammarian and author who
undertook a holistic reform of education for girls
and women that valorized women's intellectual
capabilities and argued that serious education for all
women would result in greater social and economic
opportunities for themselves, for their families and
for society as a whole.

LESSON 1:
ON CHEERFULNESS

I look on cheerfulness As on health of virtue —Young

I have always preferred cheerfulness to mirth. The latter I consider as an act, the former as a habit of the mind. Mirth is short and transient; cheerfulness fixed and permanent. Those are often raised into the greatest transports of mirth, who are subject to the greatest depressions of melancholy. On the contrary, cheerfulness, though it does not give the mind such an exquisite gladness, prevents us from falling into any depths of sorrow. Mirth is like a flash of lightning, that breaks through a gloom of clouds, and glitters for a moment; cheerfulness keeps up a kind of daylight in the mind, and fills it with a steady and perpetual serenity.

Men of austere principles look upon mirth as too wanton and dissolute for a state of probation, and as filled with a certain triumph and insolence of heart that is consistent with a life which is every moment obnoxious to the greatest dangers. Writers of this complexion have observed, that the sacred Person, who was the great pattern of perfection, was never then seen to laugh.

Cheerfulness of mind is not liable to any of these exceptions: it is of a serious and composed nature, it does not throw the mind into a condition improper for the present state of humanity, and is very conspicuous in the character of those who are looked upon as the greatest philosophers among the heathens, as well as among those who have been deservedly esteemed as saints and holy men among Christians.

If we consider cheerfulness in three lights, with regard to ourselves, to those we converse with, and to the great Author of our being, it will not a little recommend itself on each of those accounts. The man who is possessed of this excellent frame of mind, is not only easy in his thoughts, but a perfect master of all the powers and faculties of his soul: his imagination is always clear, and his judgment undisturbed: his temper is even and unruffled, whether in action or solitude: He comes with a relish of all those goods which nature has provided for him, tastes all the pleasures of the creation which are poured about him, and does not feel the full weight of those accidental evils which may befall him.

If we consider him in relation to the persons whom he converses with, it naturally produces love and good-will towards him. A cheerful mind is not only disposed to be affable and obliging, but raises the same good humour in those who come within its influence. A man finds himself pleased, he does not know why, with the cheerfulness of his companions: it is like a sudden sun-shine that awakens a secret delight in the mind without attending to it. The heart rejoices of its own accord, and naturally flows out into friendship and benevolence towards the person who has so kindly an effect upon it.

When I consider this cheerful state of mind in its third relation, I cannot but look upon it as a constant habitual gratitude to the great Author of nature. And inward cheerfulness is an implicit praise and thanksgiving to Providence under its dispensations. It is a kind of acquiescence in the state wherein we are placed, and a secret approbation of the divine will in his conduct towards man.

There are but two things, which, in my opinion, can reasonably deprive us of this cheerfulness of heart. The first of these is the sense of guilt. A man who lives in a state of vice and impenitence, can have no title to the evenness and tranquility of mind, which is the health of the soul, and the natural effect of virtue and innocence. Cheerfulness in an ill man deserves a harder name than language can furnish us with, and as many degrees beyond what we commonly call folly and madness.

Atheism, by which I mean a disbelief of the Supreme Being, and consequently of a future state, under whatsoever title it shelters itself, may likewise very reasonably deprive a man of his cheerfulness of temper. There is something so particularly gloomy and offensive to human nature in the prospect of non-existence, that I cannot but wonder, with many excellent writers, how it is possible for a man to out-live the expectation of it. For my own part, I think the being of a God is so little to be doubted, that it is almost the only truth we are sure of, and such a truth as we meet with in every object, in every occurrence, and in every thought. If we look into the character of this tribe of infidels, we generally find, they are made up of pride, spleen, and cavil. It is indeed no wonder, that men, who are uneasy to themselves, should be so to the rest of the world; and how is it possible for a man to be otherwise than uneasy in himself, when he is in danger every moment of losing his entire existence, and dropping into nothing!

The vicious man and Atheist have therefore no pretense to cheerfulness, and would act very unreasonably, should they endeavor at it. It is impossible for anyone to live in good humor, and enjoy his present existence, who is apprehensive either of torment, or annihilation; of being miserable, or of not being at all.

After having mentioned these two great principles which are destructive of cheerfulness in their own nature, as well as in right reason, I cannot think of any other that ought to banish this happy temper from a virtuous mind. Pain and sickness, shame and reproach, poverty and old age, nay death itself, considering the shortness of their duration, and the advantage we may reap from them, do not deserve the name of evils. A good mind may bear up under them with fortitude, with patience, and with cheerfulness of heart. The tossing of a tempest, does not discompose him, who is sure it will bring him to a joyful harbor.

A man who uses his best endeavors to live according to the dictates of virtue and right reason, has two perpetual sources of cheerfulness; in the consideration of his own nature, and of that Being on whom he has a dependence. If he look into himself, he cannot but rejoice in that existence, which is so lately bestowed upon him, and which, after millions of ages, will be still new, and still in its beginning. How many self-congratulations naturally arise in the mind when it reflects on this its entrance into eternity, when it takes a view of those improvable faculties, which in a few years, and even at his first setting out, have made so considerable a progress, and which will be still receiving an increase of perfection, and consequently an increase of happiness! The consciousness of such a Being spreads a perpetual diffusion of joy through the soul of a virtuous man, and makes him look upon himself every moment as more happy than he knows how to conceive.

The second source of cheerfulness to a good mind, is its consideration of that Being on whom we have our dependence, and in whom, though we behold him, as yet but in the first faint discoveries of his perfections, we see everything that we can imagine as great, glorious, or amiable. We find ourselves everywhere upheld by his goodness, and surrounded with an immensity of love and mercy. In short, we depend upon a Being, whose power qualifies him to make us happy by an infinity of means, whose goodness and truth engage him to make those happy who desire it of him, and whose unchangeableness will secure us in this happiness to all eternity.

Such considerations, which everyone should perpetually cherish in his thoughts, will banish from us all that secret heaviness of heart, which unthinking men are subject to when they lie under no real afflictions; all that anguish which we may feel from any evil that actually oppresses us, to which I may likewise add, those little cracklings of mirth and folly that are more apt to betray virtue than support it; and establish in us such an even and cheerful temper, as will make us pleasing to ourselves, to those with whom we converse, and to him whom we were made to please.

LESSON 2:

ON HAPPINESS

Know then this truth—enough for man to know,
Virtue alone is happiness below.
—Pope

I ought hourly to be looking up with gratitude and praise to the Creator of my being, for having formed me of a disposition that throws off every particle of spleen, and either directs my attention to objects of cheerfulness and joy, or enables me to look upon their contraries as I do on shades in a picture, which add force to the lights, and beauty to the whole. With this happiness of constitution I can behold the luxury of the times, as giving food and clothing to the hungry and the naked; extending our commerce, and promoting and encouraging the liberal arts. I can look upon the horrors of war, as productive of the blessings and enjoyments of peace; and upon the miseries of mankind, which I cannot relieve, with a thankful heart that my own lot has been more favorable.

There is a passage in that truly original poem, called the Spleen which pleases me more than almost anything I have read. The passage is this:

Happy the man who innocent,

Grieves not at ills he can't prevent;

His skiff does with the current glide,

Nor puffing pull'd against the tide:

He, paddling by the scuffling crowd,

Sees unconcern'd life's wager row'd;

And when he can't prevent foul play,

Enjoys the follies of the fray.

(Editor's note: The Spleen was written by Matthew Green (1697-1737). In addition to Fisher's praise, this poem also earned the praise of Pope and Gray.)

The laughing philosopher has always appeared to me a more eligible character than the weeping one: but before I sit down either to laugh or to cry at the follies of mankind, as I have publicly enlisted myself in their service, it becomes me to administer everything in my power to relieve or cure them. For this purpose I shall here lay before my readers some loose hints on a subject, which will, I hope, excite their attention, and contribute towards the expelling from the heart those malignant and sullen humours, which destroy the harmony of social life.

If we make observations on human nature, either from what we feel in ourselves, or see in others, we shall perceive that almost all the uneasiness of mankind owe their rise to inactivity or idleness of body or mind. A free and brisk circulation of the blood is absolutely necessary towards the creating easiness and good humour; and is the only means of securing us from a restless train of idle thoughts, which cannot fail to make us burthensome to ourselves, and dissatisfied with all about us.

Providence has therefore wisely provided for the generality of mankind, by compelling them to use that labor which not only procures them the necessaries of life, but peace and health to enjoy them with delight. Nay farther, we find how essentially necessary it is that the greatest part of mankind should be obliged to earn their bread by labor, from the ill use that is almost universally made of those riches which exempt men from it. Even the advantages of the best education are generally found to be insufficient to keep us within the limits of reason and moderation. How hard do the very best of men find it, to force upon themselves that abstinence or labor which the narrowness of their circumstances does not immediately compel them to? Is there really one in ten, who, by all the advantages of wealth and leisure, is made more happy in respect to himself, or more useful to mankind? What numbers do we daily see of such persons, either rioting in luxury, or sleeping in sloth, for one who makes a proper use of the advantages, which riches give for the improvement of himself, or the happiness of others! And how many do we meet with, who, for their abuse of the blessings of life, are given up to perpetual uneasiness of mind, and to the greatest agonies of bodily pain?

Whoever seriously considers this point, will discover, that riches are by no means such certain blessings as the poor imagine them to be: on the contrary, he will perceive, that the common labors and employments of life are much better suited to the majority of mankind, than prosperity and abundance would be without them.

It was a merciful sentence which the Creator passed on man for his disobedience, *by the sweat of the face thou shalt eat thy bread*; for to the punishment itself he stands indebted for health, strength, and all the enjoyments of life. Though the first paradise was forfeited for his transgression, yet by the penalty inflicted for that transgression the earth is made into a paradise again, in the beautiful fields and gardens which we see daily produced by the labor of men.

And though the ground was pronounced cursed for his disobedience, yet is that curse so ordered, as to be the punishment, chiefly and almost solely of those, who, by intemperance of sloth, inflict it upon themselves.

Even from the wants and weaknesses of mankind are the bonds of mutual support and affection derived. The necessities of each, which no man himself can sufficiently supply, compel him to contribute towards the benefit of others; and while he labors only for his own advantage, he is promoting the universal good of all around him. Health is the blessing that every one wishes to enjoy; but the multitude are so unreasonable, as to desire to purchase it at a cheaper rate than it is to be obtained. The continuance of it is only to be secured by exercise or to overlook their own enjoyments, and to view with envy the case and affluence of their superiors, not considering that the usual attendants upon great fortunes are anxiety and disease.

If it be true, that those persons are the happiest who have the fewest wants, the rich man is more the object of compassion than envy. However moderate his inclinations may be, the custom of the world lays him under a kind of necessity of living up to his fortune. He must be surrounded by an useless train of servants: his appetite must be palled with plenty, and his peace invaded by crowds. He must give up the pleasures and endearments of domestic life, to be the slave and party of faction. Or, if the goodness of his heart should incline him to acts of humanity and benevolence, he will have the frequent mortification of seeing his charities ill bestowed; and by his inability to relieve all, the constant one of making more enemies by his refusals, than friends by his benefactions. If we add to these considerations a truth, which I believe few persons will dispute, namely, that the greatest fortunes, by adding to the wants of their possessors, usually render them the most necessitous of men, we shall find greatness and happiness to be at a wide distance from one another. If we carry our inquires still higher; if we examine into the state of a King, and even enthrone him, like our own, in the hearts of his people; if the life of a father be a life of care and anxiety, to be the father of a people is a pre-eminence to be honored, but not envied.

This happiness of life is, I believe, generally to be found in those stations, which neither totally subject men to labor, nor absolutely exempt them from it. Power is the parent of disquietude, ambition of disappointment, and riches of disease.

I will conclude these reflections with the following fable:

"Labor, the offspring of want, and the mother of Health and Contentment, lived with her two daughters in a little cottage by the side of a hill, at a great distance from town. They were totally unacquainted with the great, and had kept no better company than the neighboring villagers: but having a desire of seeing the world, they forsook their companions and habitation, and determined to travel. Labor went soberly along the road, with Health on her right hand, who, by the sprightliness of her conversation, and songs of cheerfulness and joy, softened the toils of the way; while Contentment went smiling on the left, supporting the steps of her mother, and, by her perpetual good humour, increasing the vivacity of her sister.

"In this manner they travelled over forests, and through towns and villages, till at last they arrived at the capital of the kingdom. At their entrance into the great city, the mother conjured her daughters never to lose sight of her; for it was the will of Jupiter, she said, that their separation should be attended with the utter ruin of all three; but Health was of too gay a disposition to regard the counsels of Labor: she suffered herself to be debauched by Intemperance, and at last died in childbed of Disease. Contentment, in the absence of her sister, gave herself up to the enticements of Sloth, and was never heard of after: while Labor, who could have no enjoyment without her daughters, went everywhere in search of them, till she was at last seized by a lassitude in her way, and died in misery."

LESSON 3:

THE ART OF HAPPINESS

Love, hope, and joy—fair pleasure's smiling train;
Hate, fear, and grief—the family of pain.
—Pope

A good temper is one of the principal ingredients of happiness. This, it will be said, is the work of nature, and must be born with us: and so in a good measure it is; yet oftentimes it may be acquired with art, and always improved by culture. Almost every object that attracts our notice, has its bright and its dark side: he that habituates himself to look at the displeasing side, will sour his disposition, and consequently impair his happiness; while he who constantly beholds it on the bright side, insensibly meliorates his temper, and in consequence of it, improves his own happiness, and the happiness of all about him.

Arachne and Melissa are two friends. They are both of them women in years, and alike in birth, fortune, education, and accomplishments. They were originally alike in temper too; but by different management are grown the reverse of each other. Arachne has accustomed herself to look only on the dark side of every object. If a new play or poem makes its appearance, with a thousand brilliancies, and but one or two blemishes, she slightly skims over the passages that should give her pleasure, and dwells upon those only that fill her with dislike. If you show her a very excellent portrait, she looks at some part of the drapery that has been neglected, or to a hand or finger which has been left unfinished. Her garden is a very beautiful one, and kept with great neatness and elegance; but if you take a walk with her into it, she talks to you of nothing but blights and storms, of snails and caterpillars, and how impossible it is to keep it from the litter of falling leaves, and worm casts. If you sit down in one of her temples, to enjoy a delightful prospect, she observes to you, that there is too much wood, or too little water: that the day is too sunny, or too gloomy; that it is sultry or windy; and finishes with a long harangue upon the wretchedness of our climate. When you return with her to the company, in hopes of a cheerful conversation, she casts a gloom over all, by giving you the history of her own bad health, or of some melancholy accident that has befallen one of her daughter's children. Thus, she insensibly sinks her own spirits, and the spirits of all around her, and at last discovers, she knows not why, that her friends are grave.

Melissa is the reverse of all this. By constantly habituating herself to look only on the bright side of objects, she preserves a perpetual cheerfulness in herself, which, by a kind of happy contagion, she communicates to all about her. If any misfortune has befallen her, she considers it might have been worse, and is thankful to Providence for an escape. She rejoices in solitude, as it gives her an opportunity of knowing herself; and in society, because she can communicate the happiness she enjoys. She opposes every man's virtues to his failings, and can find out something to cherish and applaud in the very worst of her acquaintance. She opens every book with a desire to be entertained or instructed, and therefore seldom misses what she looks for. Walk with her, though it be but on a heath or a common, and she will discover numberless beauties unobserved before in the hills, the dales, the brooks, brakes, and the variegated flowers of weeds and poppies. She enjoys every change of weather and of season, as bringing with it something of health or convenience. In conversation, it is a rule with her, never to start a subject that leads to anything gloomy or disagreeable; you therefore never hear her repeating her own grievances, or those of her neighbors, or (what is worst of all) their faults and imperfections. If anything of the latter kind be mentioned in her hearing, she has the address to turn it into entertainment, by changing the most odious railing into pleasant raillery. Thus Melissa, like the bee, gathers honey from every weed; while Arachne, like the spider, sucks poison from the fairest flowers. The consequence is, that of two tempers, once very nearly allied, the one is forever sour and dissatisfied, the one spreads an universal gloom; the other a continual sunshine.

There is nothing more worthy of our attention than this are of happiness. In conversation as well as life, happiness very often depends upon the slightest incidents. The taking notice of the badness of the weather, a north-east wind, the approach of winter, or any trifling circumstance of the disagreeable kind, shall insensibly rob a whole company of its good humor, and fling every member of it into the vapors. If, therefore, we would be happy in ourselves, and are desirous of communicating that happiness to all about us, these minutiae of conversation ought carefully to be attended to. The brightness of the sky, the lengthening of the days, the increasing verdure of the spring, the arrival of any little piece of good news, or whatever carries with it the most distant glimpse of joy, shall frequently be the parent of a social and happy conversation. Good manners exact from us this regard for our company. The clown may repine at the sunshine that ripens his harvest, because his turnips are burnt up by it; but the man of refinement will extract pleasure from the thunder storm to which he is exposed, by remarking on the plenty and refreshment which may be expect from such a shower.

Thus does good manners, as well as good sense, direct us to look at every object on the bright side; and by thus acting, we cherish and improve both the one and the other. By this practice it is that Melissa is become the wisest and the best-bred woman living; and by this practice may every man and woman arrive at that easy benevolence of temper, which the world calls Good Nature, and the scripture Charity, whose natural and never-failing fruit is Happiness.

LESSON 4:

ON BEAUTY AND FLATTERY

Beauties, like Princes, from their very youth,
Are perfect strangers to the voice of truth.
—Pope

A friend of mine has two daughters, whom I shall call Laetitia and Daphne; the former is one of the greatest beauties of the age in which she lives, the latter no way remarkable for any charms in her person. Upon this one circumstance of their outward form, the good and ill of their lives seemed to turn. Laetitia has not, from her very childhood, heard anything else but commendations of her features and complexion, by which means she is no other than nature made her, a very beautiful outside. The consciousness of her charms has rendered her insupportably vain and insolent towards all who have to do with her. Daphne, who was almost twenty before one civil thing had ever been said to her, found herself obliged to acquire some accomplishments to make up for the want of those attractions which she saw in her sister. Poor Daphne was seldom submitted to in a debate wherein she was concerned; her discourse had nothing to recommend it but the good sense of it; and she was always under a necessity to have very well considered what she was to say, before she uttered it; while Laetitia was listened to with partiality, and approbation sat on the countenances of those she conversed with, before she communicated what she had to say.

These causes have produced suitable effects, and Laetitia is as insipid a companion as Daphne is an agreeable one. Laetitia, confident of favor, has studied no arts to please. Daphne, despairing of any inclination towards her person, has depended only on her merit. Laetitia has always something in her air that is sullen, grave, and disconsolate. Daphne has a countenance that appears cheerful, open, and unconcerned.

A young gentleman saw Laetitia this winter at a play, and became her captive. His fortune was such, that he wanted very little introduction to speak his sentiments to her father. The lover was admitted with the utmost freedom into the family, where a constrained behavior, severe looks, and distant civilities, were the highest favors he could obtain of Laetitia; while Daphne used him with the good humor, familiarity, and innocence of a sister: insomuch, that he would often say to her, dear Daphne, were thou but as handsome as Laetitia!—She received such language with that ingenuous and pleasing mirth which is natural to a woman without design. He still sighed in vain for Laetitia, but found certain relief in the agreeable conversation of Daphne. At length, heartily tired with the haughty impertinence of Laetitia, and charmed with the repeated instances of good humor he had observed in Daphne, he one day told the latter, that he had something to say to her he hoped she would be pleased with. — *Faith, Daphne,* continued he, *I am in love with thee, and despise thy sister sincerely.* — The manner of his declaring himself gave his mistress occasion for a very hearty laughter. — *Nay,* says, says he, *I knew you would laugh at me, but I will ask your father.* He did so: the father received his intelligence with no less joy than surprise, and was very glad he had now no care left but for his beauty, which he thought he could carry to market at leisure.

I do not know anything that has pleased me so much a great while, as the conquest of my friend Daphne's. All her acquaintances congratulate her upon her chance medley, and laugh at the premeditating murder, her sister. As it is an argument of a light mind, to think the worst of ourselves for the imperfections of our persons, it is equally below us to value ourselves upon the advantages of them. The female world seem to be almost incorrigibly gone astray in this particular; for which reason I shall recommend the following extract out of a friend's letter to the Professed Beauties, who are a people almost as insufferable as the Professed Wits.

"Monsieur St. Evremont has concluded one of his essays with affirming, that the last sighs of a handsome woman are not so much for the loss of her life as of her beauty. Perhaps this raillery is pursued too far, yet it is turned upon a very obvious remark, that a woman's strongest passion is for her own beauty, and that she values it as her favorite distinction. From hence it is, that all arts, which pretend to improve or preserve it, meet with so general a reception among the sex. To say nothing of many false helps, and contraband wares of beauty, which are daily vended in this great market, there is not a maiden gentlewoman, of a good family, in any country of South Britain, who has not heard of the virtue of Maydew, or is unfurnished with some receipt or other in favor of her complexion: and I have known a physician of learning and sense, after eight years study in the university, and a course of travels into most countries in Europe, owe the first rising of his fortune to a cosmetic wash.

This has given me occasion to consider, how so universal a disposition in woman-kind, which springs from a laudable motive, the desire of pleasing, and proceeds from an opinion not altogether groundless, that nature, helped by art, may be turned to their advantage. And, methinks, it would be an acceptable service to take them out of the hands of quacks and pretenders, and to prevent their imposing upon themselves, by discovering to them the true secret and art of improving beauty.

In order to do this, before I touch upon it directly, it will be necessary to lay down a few preliminary maxims, viz.

That no woman can be handsome by the force of features alone, any more than she can be witty only by the help of speech.

That pride destroys all symmetry and grace, and affectation is a more terrible enemy to fine faces than the smallpox.

That no woman is capable of being beautiful who is not incapable of being false....

From these few principles, thus laid down, it will be easy to prove, that the true art of assisting beauty, consists in embellishing the whole person, by the proper ornaments of virtuous and commendable qualities. By this help alone it is, that those who are the favorite work of nature, or, as Mr. Dryden expresses it, the porcelain clay of humankind, become animated, and are in a capacity of exerting their charms; and those who seem to have been neglected by her, like models wrought in haste, are capable, in a great measure, of finishing what she has left imperfect.

It is, methinks, a low and degrading idea of that sex, which was created to refine the joys, and soften the cares of humanity, by the most agreeable participation, to consider them merely as objects of sight. This is abridging them of their natural extent of power, to put them upon a level with their pictures at Knellers's. How much nobler is the contemplation of beauty heightened by virtue, and commanding our esteem and love, while it draws our observation! How faint and spiritless are the charms of a coquette, when compared with the real loveliness of Sophronia's innocence, piety, good-humor, and truth; virtues which add a new softness to her sex, and even beautify her beauty! (Editor's note: The name Sophronia is a girl's name of Greek origin meaning "sensible, prudent".) That agreeableness, which must otherwise have appeared no longer in the modest virgin, is now preserved in the tender mother, the prudent friend, and the faithful wife. Colors artfully spread upon canvas, may entertain the ye, but not affect the heart; and she who takes no care to add to the natural graces of her person any excellent qualities, may be allowed still to amuse as a picture, but not to triumph as a beauty.

When Adam is introduced by Milton, describing Eve in Paradise, and relating to the Angel the impressions he felt upon seeing her at her first creation, he does not represent her like a Grecian Venus, by her shape or features, but by the luster of her mind which shone in them, and gave them their power of charming:

> *Grace was in all her steps, Heav'n in her eye,*
> *In every gesture dignity and love.*

Without this irradiating power, the proudest fair one ought to know, whatever her glass may tell her to the contrary, that her most perfect features are uninformed and dead.

I cannot better close this moral, than by a short epitaph written by Ben Johnson, with a spirit which nothing could inspire but such an object as I have been describing."

> *Underneath this stone doth lie*
> *As much Virtue as could die:*
> *Which, when alive, did vigor give*
> *To as much beauty as could live.*

LESSON 5:
A HYMN

THESE, as they change, Almighty Father! These
Are but the varied God. The rolling year
Is full of thee. Forth in the pleasing Spring
Thy beauty walks, thy tenderness and love.
Wide flush the fields, the soft'ning air is balm;
Echo the mountains round; the forest smiles'
And every sense, and every heart is joy.
Then comes thy glory in the Summer months,
With light and heat refulgent. Then thy sun
Shoots full perfection through the swelling year;
And oft thy voice in dreadful thunder speaks;
And oft at dawn, deep noon, or falling eve,
By brooks and groves in hollow whispering gales
Thy bounty shines in autumn unconfin'd,
And spreads a common feast for all that live.
In Winter, awful Thou! with clouds and storms
Around Thee thrown, tempest o'er tempest roll'd
Majestic darkness on the whirlwind's wings
Riding sublime, Thou bidst the world adore,
And humblest nature with thy northern blast.

Mysterious mind! what skill, what force divine,

Deep felt in these appear! A simple train,

Yet so delightful mix'd, with such kind art,

Such beauty and beneficence combin'ed,

Shade, unperceiv'd, so soft'ning into shade

And all so forming an harmonious whole,

That, as they still succeed, they ravish still.

But wand'ring oft, with brute unconscious gaze,

Man marks not Thee, marks not the mighty hand,

That, ever busy, wheels the silent spheres;

Works in the secret deep, shoots, streaming thence

The fair profusion that o'erspreads the Spring;

Flings from the sun direct the flaming day;

Fuels every creature, hurls the tempest forth;

And, as on earth this grateful change revolves,

With transport touches all the springs of life.

Nature, attend! join, every living soul

Beneath the spacious temple of the sky:

In adoration join; and, ardent, raise

One general song! To him, ye vocal gales,

Breathe soft, whose spirit in your freshness breathes:

O talk of him in solitary glooms!

Where, o'er the rock, the scarcely waving pine

Fills the brown shade with a religious awe.

And ye, whose bolder note is heard afar,

Who shake th' astonished world, lift high to heav'n

Th' impetuous song, and say from whom ye rage.

His praise, ye brooks, attune; ye trembling rills;

And let me catch it as I muse along.

Ye headlong torrents, rapid and profound;

Ye softer floods, that lead the humid maze

Along the vale: and thou, majestic main,

A secret world of wonders in thyself,

Sound his stupendous praise; whose greater voice

Or bids you roar, or bids your roarings fall.

Soft roll your incense, herbs, and fruits and flow'rs,

In mingled clouds to him; whose sun exalts,

Whose breath perfumes you, and whose pencil paints:

Ye forests, bend; ye harvests, wave to him;

Breathe your still song into the reaper's heart,

As home he goes beneath the joyous moon.

Ye that keep watch in heav'n, as earth asleep

Unconscious lies, effuse your mildest beams.

Ye constellations, while your angels strike,

Amid the spangled sky, the silver lyre:

Great source of Day! best image here below

Of the Creator, ever pouring wide

From world to world, the vital ocean round

On nature write with every beam his praise

The thunder rolls: be hush'd the prostrate world:

While cloud to cloud retains the solemn hymn.

Bleat out afresh, ye hills; ye mossy rocks,

Retain the sound: the broad responsive low,

Ye valleys raise; for the Great Shepherd reigns;

And his unsuff'ring kingdom yet will come.

Ye woodlands all, awake: a boundless son

Burst from the groves; and when the restless day,

Expiring, lays the warbling world asleep,

Sweetest of birds! sweet Philomela, charm

The listening shades, and teach the night his praise.

Ye chief, for whom the whole creation smiles,

At once the head, the heart, and tongue of all,

Crown the great hymn! in the swarming cities vast,

Assembled men, to the deep organ join

The long resounding voice, oft breaking clear,

At solemn pauses, through the swelling base;

And, as each mingling flame increases each,

In one united ardor rise to heav'n:

Or, if you rather choose the rural shade,

And find a fane in every sacred grove,

There let the shepherd's flute, the virgin lay,

The prompting seraph, and the poet's lyre,

Still sing the God of seasons as they roll.

For mc, when I forget the darling theme,

Whether the blossoms blow, the Summer ray

Russets the plain, inspiring Autumn gleams,

Or Winter rises the black'ning east,

Be my tongue mute, my fancy paint no more,

And, dead to joy, forget my heart to beat!

Should fate command me to the farthest verge

Of the green earth, to distant barb'rous climes,

Rivers unknown to song; where first the sun

Gilds Indian mountains, or his setting beam

Flames on th' Atlantic isles; 'tis naught to me:

Since God is ever present, ever felt,

In the void waste, as in the city full;

And where he vital breathes, there must be joy.

When ev'n at last the solemn hours shall come,

And wing my mystic flight to future worlds,

I cheerful will obey. There with new powers,

Will rising wonders sing: I cannot go

Where universal love not smiles around,

Sustaining all you orbs and all their suns,

From seeming evil still educing good,

And better thence again, and better still,

In infinite progression. — But I lose

Myself in HIM, in LIGHT INEFABLE!

Come then, expressive Silence, muse his praise.

LESSON 6:
THE FABLE OF
THE FOX AND THE CAT

THE Fox and the Cat, as they travell'd one day,

With moral discourses cut shorter the way;

'Tis great, says the Fox, to make justice our guide:'

'How godlike is mercy!' Grimalkin reply'd.

While thus they proceeded, a wolf from the wood,

Impatient of hunger, and thirsting for blood,

Rushed forth—as he saw the dull shepherd asleep,

And siez'd for his supper an innocent sheep.

In vain, wretched victim, for mercy you bleat,

When mutton's at hand, says the wolf, I must eat.

Grimalkin's astonish'd—The Fox stood aghast,

To see the fell beast at his bloody repast.

'What a wretch, says the Cat— 'tis the vilest of brutes:

'Does he feed upon flesh, when there's herbage & roots?'

Cries the Fox— 'While our oaks give us acorns so good,'

'What a tyrant is this, to spill innocent blood?'

Well, onward they march'd, and they moraliz'd still,

Till they came where some poultry pick'd chaff by a mill:

Sly Reynard survey'd them with gluttonous eyes,

And made (spite of morals) a pullet his prize,

A mouse too that chanch'd from her covert to stray,

The greedy Grimalkin secur'd as her prey.

A spider that far in her web on the wall,

Perceiv'd the poor victims, and pity'd their fall;

She cry'd— Of such murders how guiltless am I!

So ran to regale on a new-taken fly.

MORAL

The faults of our neighbors with freedom we blame,

But tax not ourselves, though we practice the same.

LESSON 7:
THE UNIVERSAL PRAYER

FATHER of all! in every age,
    In every clime ador'd
By saint, by savage, and by sage,
    Jehovah, Jove, or *Lord.*

Thou Great First Cause, least understood,
    Who all my sense confin'd,
To know but this, that thou art good,
    And that myself am blind.

Yet gave me in this dark estate,
    To see the good from ill;
And binding Nature fast in fate,
    Left free the human will.

That conscience dictates to be done,
    Or warns me not do,
This teach me more than hell to shun,
    That more than heav'n pursue.

What blessings thy free bounty gives,

    Let me not cast away;

For God is paid when man receives,

    T' enjoy is to obey.

Yet not to earth's contracted span

    Thy goodness let me bound,

Or think thee Lord alone of man,

    When thousand worlds are round.

Let not this weak unknowing hand

    Presume thy bolts to throw,

O deal damnation round the land,

    On each I judge thy foe.

If I am right, O teach my heart

    Still in the right to stray:

If I am wrong, thy grace impart,

    To find the better way.

Save me alike from foolish pride,

    Or impious discontent,

At aught thy goodness deny'd,

    Or naught thy goodness lent.

Teach me to feel another's woe,

    To hide the fault I see;

That merry I to others show,

    That mercy show to me.

Mean though I am, not wholly so,

    Since quickened by thy breath:

O lead me wheresoe'er I go,

    Through this day's life or death.

This day be bread and peace my lot;

    All else beneath the sun

Thou know'st if best bestow'd, or not,

    And let thy will be done.

To thee, whose temple is all space,

    Whose altar, earth, sea, skies;

One chorus let all beings raise!

    All Nature's incense rise!

              — Alexander Pope

PART V:
SELECTED LESSONS FROM

Introduction to the English Reader

Compiled by
Lindley Murray

Halifax:
Hartley and Walker, Cheapside, 1837

LESSON 1:
THE ADVANTAGES
OF EARLY RELIGION

HAPPY the child whose tender years
   Receive instruction well;
Who hates the sinner's path, and fears
   The road that leads to hell.

When we give up our youth to God,
   'Tis pleasing in his eyes:
A flow'r, that's offer'd in the bud,
   Is no vain sacrifice.

'Tis easy work, if we begin
   To fear the Lord betimes;
While sinners, who grow old in sin,
   Are harden'd in their crimes.

'Twill save us from a thousand snares,
   To mind religion young;
It willpreserve our following years,

And make our virtue strong,

To thee, Almighty God! to thee
   Our childhood we resign;
'Twill please us to look back and see
   That our whose lives were thine.

Let the sweet work of pray'r and praise
   Employ our youngest breath;
Thus we're prepar'd for longer days,
   Or fit for early death.

—**WATTS**

LESSON 2:
THE EXCELLENCE OF THE BIBLE

GREAT God! with wonder and with praise
  On all thy works I look;
But still thy wisdom, pow'r, and grace,
  Shine brightest in thy book.

The stars, which in their courses roll,
  Have much instruction given;
But thy good word informs my soul
  How I may get to Heav'n.

The fields provide me food, and show
  The goodness of the Lord;
But fruits of life and glory grow
  In thy most holy word.

Here are my choicest treasures hid,
  Here my best comfort lies:
Here my desires are satisfied,
  And hence my hopes arise.

Lord! make me understand thy law;
> Show what my faults have been;
And from thy gospel let me draw
> Pardon for all my sin.

For her I learn how Jesus died,
> To save my soul from hell:
Not all the books on earth beside
> Such heav'nly wonders tell.

Then let me love my Bible more,
> And take a fresh delight,
By day to read these wonders o'er,
> And meditate by night.

—**WATTS**

LESSON 3:

A GENEROUS MIND DOES NOT REPINE AT THE ADVANTAGES OTHERS ENJOY

Ever charming, ever new,

When will the landscape tire the view!

The fountains' fall, the river's flow,

The woody valleys, warm and low;

The windy summit, wild and high,

Roughly rushing on the sky;

The pleasant seat, the ruin'd tow'r,

The naked rock, the shady bow'r;

The town and village, dome and farm,

Each gives to each a double charm

—**Dyer**

Alexis was repeating these lines to Euphronius, who was reclining upon a seat in one of his fields, enjoying the real beauties of nature which the poet describes. The evening was serene, and the landscape appeared in all the gay attire of light and shade. "A man of lively imagination," said Euphronius, "has a property in everything which he sees: and you may now conceive yourself to be the proprietor of the vast expanse around us; and exult in happiness of myriads of living creatures, that inhabit the woods, the lawns, and the mountains, which present themselves to our view." The house, garden, and pleasure-grounds of Eugenio formed a part of the prospect: and Alexis expressed a jocular wish, that he had more than an imaginary property in those possessions. "Banish the ungenerous desire," said Euphronius; "for if you indulge such emotions as these, your heart will soon become a prey to envy and discontent. Enjoy, with gratitude the blessings which you have received from the liberal hand of providence; increase them, if you can, with honor and credit, by a diligent attention to the business for which you are designed and though your own cup may not be filled, rejoice that your neighbor's overflows with plenty. Honor the abilities, and emulate the virtues of Eugenio: but repine not that he is wiser, richer, or more powerful than yourself. His fortune is expended in acts of humanity, generosity, and hospitality. His superior talents are applied to the instruction of his children; to the assistance of his friends; to the encouragement of agriculture, and of every useful art; and to support the cause of liberty and the rights of mankind. And his power is exerted to punish the guilty, to protect the innocent, to reward the good, and to distribute justice, with an equal hand, to all. I feel the affection of a brother for Eugenio; and esteem myself singularly happy in his friendship."

—PERCIVAL

LESSON 4:

INSOLENT DEPORTMENT TOWARDS INFERIORS REPROVED

SACCHARISSA was about fifteen years of age. Nature had given her a high spirit, and education had fostered it into pride and haughtiness. This temper was displayed in every little competition which she had with her companions. She could not brook the least opposition from those whom she regarded as her inferiors; and if they did not instantly submit to her inclination, she assumed all her airs of dignity, and treated them with the most supercilious contempt. She domineered over her father's servants; always commanding their good offices with the voice of authority, and disdaining the gentler language of request. Euphronius was one day walking with her, when the gardener brought her a nosegay which she had ordered him to collect. "Blockhead!" she cried, as he delivered it to her; "what strange flowers you have chosen; and how awkwardly you have put them together!" "Blame not the man with so much harshness," said Euphronius, "because his taste is different from yours! He meant to please you; and his good intention merits your thanks, and not your censure." "Thanks!" replied Saccharissa, scornfully. "He is paid for his services, and it is his duty to perform them." "And if he does perform, he acquits himself of his duty," returned Euphronius. "The obligation is fulfilled on his side; and you have no more right to upbraid him for executing your orders according to his best ability, than he has to claim from your father, more wages than were covenanted to be given him." "But he is a poor dependent," said Saccharissa, "and earns a livelihood by his daily labor." "That livelihood," answered Euphronius, "is the just price of his labor; and if he receive nothing further from your hands, the account is balanced between you. But a generous person compassionates the lot of those, who are obliged to toil for his benefit or gratification. He lightens their burdens; treats them with kindness and affection; studies to promote their interest and happiness; and, as much as possible, conceals from them their servitude, and his superiority. On the distinctions of rank and fortune, he does not set too high a value: and though the circumstances of his life require, that there should be hewers of wood, and drawers of water, yet he forgets not that mankind are by nature equal; all being the offspring of God, the subjects of his moral government, and joint heirs of immortality. A conduct directed by such principles, gives a master claims, which no money can purchase, no labor can repay. His affection can only be compensated by love; his kindness by gratitude; and his cordiality, by the service of the heart."

—PERCIVAL

LESSON 5:

BRETHREN SHOULD DWELL
TOGETHER IN HARMONY

Two brothers, named Cherephon and Cherecrates, having quarreled with each other, Socrates, their common friend, was solicitous to restore amity between them. Meeting, therefore, with Cherecrates, he thus accosted him: "Is not friendship the sweetest solace in adversity, and the greatest enhancement of the blessings of prosperity?" "Certainly it is," replied Cherecrates; "because our sorrows are diminished, and our joys increased by sympathetic participation." "Amongst whom, then, must we look for a friend?" said Socrates. "Would you search among strangers? They cannot be interested about you. Amongst those who are much older, or younger, than yourself? Their feelings and pursuits will be widely different from yours. Are there not, then some circumstances favorable, and others essential, to the formation of friendship?" "Undoubtedly there are," answered Cherecrates. "May we not enumerate," continued Socrates, "among the circumstances favorable to friendship, long acquaintance, common connections, similitude of age, and union of interest?" "I acknowledge," said Cherecrates, "the powerful influence of these circumstances: but they subsist, and yet others be wanting, that are essential to mutual amity." "And what," said Socrates, "are those essentials which are wanting in Cherephron?" "He has forfeited my esteem and attachment," answered Cherecrates. "And has he also forfeited the esteem and attachment of the rest of mankind?" continued Socrates. "Is he devoid of benevolence, generosity, gratitude, and other social affections?" "Far be it from me," cried Cherecrates, "to lay so heavy a charge upon him! His conduct to others, is, I believe, irreproachable; and it wounds me the more, that he should single me out as the object of his unkindness." "Suppose you have a very valuable horse," resumed Socrates, "gentle under the treatment of others, but ungovernable, when you attempt to use him; would you not endeavor, by all means, to conciliate his affection, and to treat him in the way most likely to render him tractable? Or, if you have a dog, highly prized for his fidelity, watchfulness, and care of your flocks, who is fond of your shepherds, and playful with them, and yet snarls whenever you come his way; would you attempt to cure him of this fault by angry looks or words, or by any other marks of resentment? You would surely pursue an opposite course with him. And is not the friendship of a brother of far more worth, than the services of a horse, or the attachment of a dog? Why, then, do you delay to put in practice those means, which may reconcile you to Cherephon?"—"Acquaint me with those means, answered Cherecrates, "for I am a stranger to them." "Answer me a questions," said Socrates. "If you desire that one of your neighbors should invite you to his feast, when he offers a sacrifice, what course would you take?"—"I would fist invite him to mine."—"And how would you induce him to take the charge of your affairs, when you are on a journey?"—"I should be forward to do the same good office to him in his absence."—"If you be solicitous to remove a prejudice, which he may have received against you, how would you then behave towards him?"—"I should endeavor to convince him, by my looks, words, and actions, that such prejudice was ill-founded."—"And if he appeared inclined to reconciliation, would you reproach him with the injustice he had done you?"—"No, answered Cherecrates; "I would repeat no grievances."—"Go," said Socrates, "and pursue that conduct towards your brother, which you would practice to a neighbor. His friendship is of inestimable worth; and nothing is more lovely in the sight of Heaven, than for brethren to dwell together in unity."

—PERCIVAL

LESSON 6:

DEPENDENCE ON PROVIDENCE

REGARD the world with cautious eye,

Nor raise your expectations high.

See that the balanc'd scales be such,

You neither fear nor hope too much.

For disappointment's not the thing;

'Tis pride and passion point the sting.

Life is a sea where storms must rise;

'Tis folly talks of cloudless skies:

He who contracts his swelling said,

Eludes the fury of the gale.

Be still, nor anxious thoughts employ;

Distrust embitters present joy:

On God for all events depend;

You cannot want when God's your firend.

Weigh well your part, and do your best;

Leave to your Maker all the rest.

The hand which form'd thee in the womb,

Guides from the cradle to the tomb.

Can the fond mother slight her boy;

Can she forget her prattling joy?

Say then, shall sov'reign Love desert

The humble, and the honest heart?

Heav'n may not grant thee all thy mind;

Yet say not thou that Heav'n's unkind.

God is alike, both good and wise,

In what he grants, and what denies:

Perhaps, what Goodness gives today,

Tomorrow, Goodness takes away.

You say, that troubles intervene;

That sorrows darken half the scene.

True—and this consequence you see,

The world was ne'er design'd for thee:

You're like a passenger below,

That stays perhaps a night or so;

But still his native country lies

Beyond the bound'ries of the skies.

Of Heav'n ask virtue, wisdom health;

But never let thy pray'r be wealth.

If food be thine, (tho' little gold,)

And raiment to repel the cold;

Such as may nature's wants suffice,

Not what from pride and folly rise;

If soft the motions of thy soul,

And a calm conscience crowns the whole;

And but a friend to all this store,

You can't in reason wish for more:

And if kind Heav'n this comfort brings.

'Tis more than Heav'n bestows on kings.

—**COTTON**

LESSON 7:
THE SLUGGARD

'Tis the voice of the sluggard—I heard him complain,

"You have wak'd me too soon, I must slumber again."

As the door on its hinges, so he on his bed

Turns his sides and his shoulders, and his heavy head.

"A little more sleep, and a little more slumber;"

Thus he wastes half his days, and his hours without number.

And when he gets up, he sits folding his hands,

Or walks about saunt'ring, or trifling he stands.

I pass'd by his garden, and saw the wild brier.

The thorn, and the thistle, grow broader and higher.

The clothes that hang on him are turning to rags;

And his money still wastes, till he starves or he begs.

I made him a visit, still hoping to find

He had ta'en better care for improving his mind:

He told me his dreams, talk'd of eating and drinking;

But he scarce reads his Bible, and never loves thinking.

Said I then to my heart, "Here's a lesson for me;

That man's but a picture of what I might be;

But thanks to my friends for their care in my breeding,

Who taught me betimes to love working and reading!"

—**WATTS**

LESSON 8:
HEAVENLY WISDOM

How happy is the man who hears
    Instruction's warning voice;
And who celestial Wisdom makes
    His early, only choice!

For she has treasures greater far
    Than east or west unfold;
And her reward is more secure
    Than is the gain of gold.

In her right-hand she holds to view
    A length of happy years;
And in her left, the prize of fame
    And honor bright appears.

She guides the young, with innocence,
    In pleasure's path to tread;
A crown of glory she bestows
    Upon the hoary head.

According as he labors rise,

She her rewards increase:

Her ways are ways of pleasantness,

And all her paths are peace.

—LOGAN

LESSON 9:
CHARACTER OF CHRIST

BEHOLD, where, in a mortal form,
    Appears each grace divine:
The virtues, all in Jesus met,
    With mildest radiance shine.

The noblest love of human-kind
    Inspir'd his holy breast;
In deeds of mercy, words of peace,
    His kindness was expressed.

To spread the rays of heavenly light,
    To give the mourner joy,
To preach glad tidings to the poor,
    Was his divine employ.

Lowly in heart, by all his friends,
    A friend and servant found;
He wash'd their feet, he wip'd their tears,
    And heal'd each bleeding wound.

Midst keen reproach, and cruel scorn,

Patient and meek he stood:

His foes, ungrateful, sought his life;

He labor'd for their good.

In the last hour of deep distress,

Before his Father's throne,

With soul resign'd, he bow'd, and said,

"Thy will, not mine, be done!"

Be Christ my pattern, and my guide!

His image may I bear!

O may I tread his sacred steps!

And his bright glories share!

—ENFIELD

LESSON 10:
LOVE TO ENEMIES

When Christ, among the sons of men,
　　In humble form was found,
With cruel slanders, false and vain,
　　He was encompass'd round.

The woes of men, his pity mov'd;
　　Their peace, he still pursu'd;
They render'd hatred for his love,
　　And evil for his good.

Their malice raged without a cause,
　　Yet, with his dying breath,
He pray'd for murd'rers on his cross,
　　And bless'd his foes in death.

From the rich fountain of his love,
　　What streams of mercy flow
"Father, forgive them," Jesus cries,
　　"They know not what they do."

Let not this bright example shine

In vain before our eyes!

Give us, great God, a soul like his,

To love our enemies.

—WATTS

LESSON 11:
A MORNING HYMN

My God, who makes the sun to know
 His proper hour to rise,
And to give light to all below,
 Does send him round the skies.

When from the chambers of the east
 His morning race begins,
He never tires, nor stops to rest:
 But round the world he shines.

So, like the sun, would I fulfill
 The business of the day:
Begin my work betimes, and still
 March on my heav'nly way.

Give me, O Lord, thy early grace,
 Nor let my soul complain,
That the young morning of my days
 Has all been spent in vain.

—WATTS

LESSON 12:
AN EVENING HYMN

And now another day is gone,
      I'll sing my Maker's praise:
My comforts ev'ry hour make known
      His providence and grace.

But how my childhood runs to waste!
      My sins, how great their sum!
Lord! give me pardon for the past,
      And strength for days to come.

I lay my body down to sleep;
      Let angels guard my head,
And through the hours of darkness keep
      Their watch around my bed.

With cheerful heart I close my eyes,
      Since God will not remove;
And in the morning let me rise,
      Rejoicing in his love.

—WATTS

PART VI:
SELECTED LESSONS FROM

The English Reader: or,
Pieces in Prose and Poetry

Compiled by
Lindley Murray

Brattleborough:
Printed by W. Fessenden for Isaiah Thomas, Jun., 1805.

LESSON 1:

THE IMPORTANCE
OF A GOOD EDUCATION

I consider a human soul, without education, like marble in the quarry; which shows none of its inherent beauties, until the skill of the polisher fetches out the colors, makes the surface shine, and discovers every ornamental cloud, spot, and vein, that runs through the body of it. Education, after the same manner, when it works upon a noble mind, draws out to view every latent virtue and perfection, which, without such helps, are never able to make their appearance.

If my reader will give me leave to change the allusion too soon upon him, I shall make use of the same instance too soon upon him, I shall make use of the same instance to illustrate the force of education, which Aristotle has brought to explain his doctrine of substantial forms, when he tells us that a statue lies hid in a block of marble; and that the art of the statuary only clears away the superfluous matter, and removes the rubbish. The figure is in the stone, and the sculptor only finds it. What sculpture is, to a block of marble, education is to a human soul. The philosopher, the saint, or the hero, the wise, the good, or the great man, very often lies hid and concealed in a plebeian, which a property education might have disinterred, and have brought to sight. I am therefore much delighted with reading the accounts of savage nations; and with contemplating those virtues which are wild and uncultivated; to see courage exerting itself in fierceness, resolution in obstinacy, wisdom in cunning, patience in sullenness and despair.

Men's passions operate variously, and appear in different kinds of actions, according as they are more or less rectified and swayed by reason. When one hears of slaves, who upon the death of their masters, or upon changing their service, hang themselves upon the next tree… who can forbear admiring their fidelity, though it expresses itself in so dreadful a manner? What might not that savage greatness of soul, which appears in these poor wretches on many occasions, be raised to, were it rightly cultivated? And what color of excuse can there be, for the contempt with which we treat this part of our species; that we should not put them upon the common foot of humanity; that we should only set an insignificant fine upon the man who murders them; nay, that we should… cut them off from the prospects of happiness in another world, as well as in this; and deny them that which we look upon as the proper means for attaining it!

It is therefore an unspeakable blessing, to be born in those parts of the world where wisdom and knowledge flourish; though it must be confessed, there are, even in these parts, several poor uninstructed persons who are but little above the inhabitants of those nations of which I have been here speaking; as those who have had the advantages of a more liberal education, rise above one another by several different degrees of perfection. For, to return to our statue in the block of marble, we see it sometimes only begun to be chipped,

144

sometimes rough-hewn, and but just sketched into a human figure; sometimes, we see the man appearing distinctly in all his limbs and features; sometimes we find the figure wrought up to great elegancy; but seldom meet with any to which the hand of a Phidias or a Praxiteles could not give several nice touches and finishing.

—ADDISON

LESSON 2:
ON GRATITUDE

There is not a more pleasing exercise of the mind, than gratitude. It is accompanied with such inward satisfaction that the duty, is sufficiently rewarded by the performance. It is not, like the practice of many other virtues, difficult and painful, but attended with so much pleasure that were there no positive command which enjoined it, nor any recompense laid up for it hereafter, a generous mind would indulge in it, for the natural gratification which it affords.

If gratitude is due from man to man, how much more from man to his Maker? The Supreme Being does not only confer upon us those bounties which proceed more immediately from his hand, but even those benefits which are conveyed to us by others. Every blessing we enjoy, by what means soever it may be derived upon us, is the gift of him who is the great Author of good, and the Father of mercies.

If gratitude, when exerted towards one another, naturally produces a very pleasing sensation in the mind of a grateful man, it exalts the soul into rapture, when it is employed on this great object of gratitude; on this beneficent Being who has given us everything we already possess and from whom we expect everything we yet hope for.

--ADDISON

LESSON 3:
ON FORGIVENESS

The most plain and natural sentiments of equity concur with divine authority, to enforce the duty of forgiveness. Let him who has never in his life done wrong, be allowed the privilege of remaining inexorable. But let such as are conscious of frailties and crimes, consider forgiveness as a debt which they owe to others. Common failings are the strongest lesson of mutual forbearance. Were this virtue unknown among men, order and comfort, peace and repose, would be strangers to human life. Injuries retaliated according to the exorbitant measure which passion prescribes, would excite resentment in return. The injured person would become the injurer; and thus wrongs, retaliations and fresh injuries, would circulate in endless succession, 'til the world was rendered a field of blood. Of all the passions which invade the human breast, revenge is the most direful. When allowed to reign with full dominion, it is more than sufficient to poison the few pleasures which remain to man in his present state. How much soever a person may suffer from injustice, he is always hazard of suffering more from the prosecution of revenge. The violence of an enemy cannot inflict what is equal to the torment he creates to himself, by means of the fierce and desperate passions which he allows to rage in his soul.

Those evil spirits who inhabit the regions of misery, are represented as delighting in revenge and cruelty. But all that is great and good in the universe, is on the side of clemency and mercy. The almighty Ruler of the world, though for ages offended by the unrighteousness, and insulted by the impiety of men, is "long suffering and slow to anger." His Son, when he appeared in our nature, exhibited, both in his life and his death, the most illustrious example of forgiveness which the world ever beheld. If we look into the history of mankind, we shall find that, in every age, they who have been respected as worthy, or admired as great, have been distinguished for this virtue. Revenge dwells in little minds. A noble and magnanimous spirit is always superior to it. It suffers not from the injuries of men those severe shocks which others feel. Collected within itself, it stands unmoved by their impotent assaults; and with generous pity, rather than with anger, looks down on their unworthy conduct. It has been truly said, that the greatest man on earth can no sooner commit an injury, than a good man can make himself greater, by forgiving it.

—**BLAIR**

LESSON 4:

MOTIVES TO THE PRACTICE
OF GENTLENESS

To promote the virtue of gentleness, we ought to view our character with an impartial eye; and to learn, from our own failings, to give that indulgence which in our turn we claim. It is pride which fills the world with so much harshness and severity. In the fullness of self-estimation, we forget what we are. We claim attentions to which we are not entitled. We are rigorous to offences, as if we had never offended; unfeeling to distress, as if we knew not what it was to suffer. From those airy regions of pride and folly, let us descend to our proper level. Let us survey the natural equality on which Providence has placed man with man, and reflect on the infirmities common to all. If the reflection on natural equality and mutual offences, be insufficient to prompt humanity, let us at least remember what we are in the sight of our Creator. Have we none of that forbearance to give one another, which we all so earnestly entreat from heaven? Can we look for clemency or gentleness from our Judge, when we are so backward to shew it to our own brethren?

Let us also accustom ourselves, to reflect on the small moment of those things, which are the usual incentives to violence and contention. In the ruffled and angry hour, we view every appearance through a false medium. The most inconsiderable point of interest, or honor swells into a momentous object; and the slightest attack seems to threaten immediate ruin. But after passion or pride has subsided, we look around in vain for the mighty mischiefs we dreaded. The fabric, which our disturbed imagination had reared, totally disappears. But though the cause of contention has dwindled away, its consequences remain. We have alienated a friend; we have embittered an enemy; we have sown the seeds of future suspicion, malevolence, or disgust. Let us suspend our violence for a moment, when cause of discord occur. Let us anticipate that period of coolness, which, of itself, will soon arrive. Let us reflect how little we have any prospect of gaining by fierce contention; but how much of the true happiness of life we are certain of throwing away. Easily, and from the smallest chink, the bitter waters of strife are let forth; but their course cannot be foreseen; and he seldom fails of suffering most from their poisonous effect, who first allowed them to flow.

—BLAIR

LESSON 5:
A SUSPICIOUS TEMPER A SOURCE OF MISERY TO ITS POSSESSOR

As a suspicious spirit is the source of many crimes and calamities in the world, so it is the spring of certain misery to the person who indulges it. His friends will be few; small will be his comfort in those whom he possesses. Believing others to be his enemies, he will of course make them such. Let his caution be ever so great, the asperity of his thoughts will often break out in his behavior; and in return for suspecting and hating, he will incur suspicion and hatred. Besides the external evils which he draws upon himself, arising from alienated friendship, broken confidence, and open enmity, the suspicious temper itself is one of the worst evils which any man can suffer. If "in all fear there is torment," how miserable must be his state, who, by living in perpetual jealousy, lives in perpetual dread! Looking upon himself to be surrounded with spies, enemies, and designing men, he is a stranger to reliance and truth. He knows not to whom to open himself. He dresses his countenance in forced smiles, while his heart throbs within from apprehensions of secret treachery. Hence fretfulness and ill humor, disgust at the world, and all the painful sensations of an irritated and embittered mind.

So numerous and great are the evils arising from a suspicious disposition, that, of the two extremes, it is more eligible to expose ourselves to occasional disadvantage from thinking too well of others, than to suffer continual misery by thinking always ill of them. It is better to be sometimes imposed upon, than never to trust. Safety is purchased at too dear a rate, when, in order to secure it, we are obliged to be always clad in armor, and to live in perpetual hostility with our fellows. This is, for the sake of living, to deprive ourselves of the comfort of life. The man of candor enjoys his situation, whatever it is, with cheerfulness and peace. Prudence directs his intercourse with the world; but no black suspicions haunt his hours of rest. Accustomed to view the characters of his neighbors in the most favorable light, he is like one who dwells amidst those beautiful scenes of nature, on which the eye rests with pleasure. Whereas the suspicious man, having his imagination filled with all the shocking forms of human falsehood, deceit, and treachery, resembles the traveler in the wilderness, who discerns no objects around him but such as are either dreary or terrible; caverns that open, serpents that hiss, and beasts of prey that howl.

—**BLAIR**

LESSON 6:
COMFORTS OF RELIGION

There are many who have passed the age of youth and beauty; who have resigned the pleasures of that smiling season; who begin to decline into the vale of years, impaired in their health, depressed in their fortunes, stripped of their friends, their children, and perhaps still more tender connections, what resource can this world afford them? It presents a dark and dreary desert, through which there does not issue a single ray of comfort. Every delusive prospect of ambition is now at an end; long experience of mankind, an experience very different from what the open and generous soul of youth had fondly dreamt of, has rendered the heart almost inaccessible to new friendships. The principal sources of activity are taken away, when those for whom we labor are cut off from us; those who animated, and those who sweetened all the toils of life. Where then can the soul find refuge, but in the bosom of Religion? Thee she is admitted to those prospects of Providence and futurity, which alone can warm and fill the heart. I speak here of such as retain the feelings of humanity; whom misfortunes have softened, and perhaps rendered more delicately sensible; not of such as possess that stupid insensibility, which some are pleased to dignify with the name of Philosophy.

It might therefore be expected, that hose philosophers, who think they stand in no need themselves of the assistance of religion to support their virtue, and who never feel the want of its consolations, would yet have the humanity to consider the very different situation of the rest of mankind; and not endeavor to deprive them of what habit, at least, if they will not allow it to be nature, has made necessary to their morals, and to their happiness. It might be expected, that humanity would prevent them from breaking into the last retreat of the unfortunate, who can no longer be objects of their envy or resentment; and tearing from them their only remaining comfort. That attempt to ridicule religion may be agreeable to some, by relieving them from restraint upon their pleasures; and may render others very miserable, by making them doubt those truths, in which they were most deeply interested; but it can convey real good and happiness to no one individual.

—GREGORY

LESSON 7:
THE DIGNITY OF VIRTUE
AMIDST CORRUPT EXAMPLES

The most excellent and honorable character which can adorn a man and a Christian, is acquired by resisting the torrent of vice, and adhering to the cause of God and virtue against a corrupted multitude. It will be found to hold in general, that all those, who, in any of the great lines of life, have distinguished themselves for thinking profoundly, and acting nobly, have despised popular prejudices; and departed, in several things, from the common ways of the world. On no occasion is this more requisite for true honor, than where religion and morality are concerned. In times of prevailing licentiousness, to maintain unblemished virtue, and uncorrupted integrity; in a public or a private cause, to stand firm by what is fair and just, amidst discouragements and opposition; despising groundless censure and reproach; disdain all compliance with public manners, when they are vicious and unlawful; and never ashamed of the punctual discharge of every duty towards God and man; this is what shows true greatness of spirit, and will force approbation even from the degenerate multitude themselves. "This is the man," (their conscience will oblige them to acknowledge,) "whom we are unable to bend to mean condescension. We see it in vain either to flatter or to threaten him; he rests on a principle within, which we cannot shake. To this man we may, on any occasion, safely commit our cause. He is incapable of betraying his trust, or deserting his friend, or denying his faith."

It is, accordingly, this steady inflexible virtue, this regard to principle, superior to all custom and opinion, which peculiarly marked the characters of those in any age, who have shone with distinguished luster; and has consecrated their memory to all posterity. It was this that obtained to ancient Enoch the most singular testimony of honor from heaven. He continued, to "walk with God," when the world apostatized from him. He pleased God, and was beloved of him; so that living among sinners, he was translated to heaven without seeing death; "Yea, speedily was he taken away, lest wickedness should have altered his understanding, or deceit beguiled his soul." When Sodom could not furnish ten righteous men to save it, Lot remained unspotted amidst the contagion. He lived like an angel among spirits of darkness; and the destroying flame was not permitted to go forth, till the good man was called away by a heavenly messenger from his devoted city. When "all flesh had corrupted their way upon the earth," then lived Noah, a righteous man, and a preacher of righteousness. He stood alone, and was scoffed by the profane crew, but they, by the deluge were swept away; while on him Providence conferred the immortal honor, of being the restorer of a better race, and the father of a new world. Such examples as these, and such honors conferred by God on them who withstood the multitude of evil doers, should often be present to our minds. Let us oppose them to the numbers of low and corrupt examples, which we behold around us; and when we are in hazard of being swayed by such, let us fortify our virtue, by thinking of those who, in former times, shone like stars in the midst of surrounding darkness, and are no shining in the kingdom of heaven, as the brightness of the firmament, for ever and ever.

—BLAIR

LESSON 8

A PARAPHRASE ON THE LATTER PART OF THE SIXTH CHAPTER OF MATTHEW

When my breast labors with oppressive care,
And o'er my cheek descends the falling tear;
While all my warring passions are at strife,
Oh! let me listen to the words of life!
Raptures deep-felt his doctrine did impart,
And thus he rais'd from earth the drooping heart.

"Think not, when all your scanty stores afford,
Is spread at once upon the sparing board;
Think not, when worn the homely robe appears,
While on the roof the howling tempest bears;
What farther shall this feeble life sustain,
And what shall clothe these shiv'ring limbs again.
Say, does not life its nourishment exceed?
And the fair body its investing weed?
Behold! and look away your low despair—
See the light tenants of the barren air:
To them, nor stores, nor granaries, belong;

Naught, but the woodland, and the pleasing song;

Yea, your kind heav'nly Father bends his eye

On the least wing that flits along the sky,

To him they sing, when spring renews the plain;

To him they cry, in winter's pinching reign;

Nor is their music, nor their plaint in vain:

He hears the gay, and the distressful call:

And with unsparing bounty fills them all."

"Observe the rising lily's snowy grace;

Observe the various vegetable race;

They neither toil, nor spin, but careless grow;

Yet see how warm they blush! how bright they glow

What regal vestments can with them compare!

What king so shining! or what queen so fair!"

"If ceaseless, thus, the fowls of heav'n he feeds;

If o'er the fields such lucid robes he spreads;

Will he not care for you, ye faithless, say?

Is he unwise? or are ye less than they?"

—**THOMSON**

LESSON 9:

A PARAPHRASE ON THE THIRTEENTH CHAPTER OF THE FIRST EPISTLE TO THE CORINTHIANS

Did sweeter sounds adorn my flowing tongue,

Than ever man pronounced or angels sung;

Had I all knowledge, human and divine,

That thought can reach, or science can define;

And had I pow'r to give that knowledge birth,

In all the speeches of the babbling earth;

Did Shadrach's zeal my glowing breast inspire,

To weary tortures, and rejoice in fire;

Or had I faith like that which Israel saw,

When Moses gave them miracles and law:

Yet gracious charity, indulgent guest,

Were not thy pow'r exerted in my breast;

Those speeches would send up unheeded pray'r;

That scorn of life would be but wild despair;

A cymbal's sound were better than my voice;

My faith were form; my eloquence were noise.

Charity, decent, modest, easy, kind,

Softens the high, and rears the abject mind;

Knows with just reins, and gentle hand, to guide

Betwixt vile shame, and arbitrary pride.

Not soon provok'd, she easily forgives;

And much she suffers, as she much believes.

Soft peace she brings whenever she arrives;

She builds our quiet, as she forms our lives;

Lays the rough paths of peevish nature even;

And opens in each heart a little heav'n.

Each other gift, which God on man bestows,

Its proper bounds and due restriction knows;

To one fix'd purpose dedicates its pow'r;

And finishing its act, exists no more.

Thus, in obedience to what Heav'n decrees,

Knowledge shall fail, and prophecy shall cease;

But lasting charity's more ample sway,

Nor bound by time, nor subject to decay,

In happy triumph shall forever live;

And endless good diffuse, and endless praise receive.

As through the artist's intervening glass,

Our eye observes the distant planets pass;

A little we discover; but allow,

That more remains unseen, than art can show;

So whilst our mind its knowledge would improve,

(Its feeble eye intent on things above,)

High as we may, we lift our reason up,

By faith directed, and confirm'd by hope;

Yet are we able only to survey

Dawnings of beams, and promises of day;

Heaven's full effluence mocks our dazzled sight;

Too great its swiftness, and too strong its light.

But soon the mediate clouds shall be dispell'd;

The sun shall soon be face to face beheld,

In all his robes, with all his glory on,

Seated sublime on his meridian throne.

Then constant faith, and holy hope shall die,

One lost in certainty, and one in joy:

Whilst thou, more happy pow'r, fair charity,

Triumphant sister, greatest of the three,

Thy office, and thy nature still the same,

Lasting thy lamp, and unconsum'd thy flame,

Shalt still survive —

Shalt stand before the host of heav'n confest,

Forever blessing, and forever blest.

—PRIOR